HERMENEUTICS AS
THEOLOGICAL PROLEGOMENA:
A CANONICAL APPROACH

Studies in American Biblical Hermeneutics 8

HERMENEUTICS AS
THEOLOGICAL PROLEGOMENA:
A CANONICAL APPROACH

by
CHARLES J. SCALISE

Mercer University Press
Macon, Georgia

ISBN: 0-86554-435-2 (paper)
        0-86554-434-4 (casebound)

Hermeneutics as Theological Prolegomena: A Canonical Approach
Charles J. Scalise
Copyright © 1994
Mercer University Press
Macon, Georgia 31207

The paper used in this publication meets the minimum
requirements of American National Standard for Information
Sciences—Permanence of Paper for Printed Library Materials,
ANSI Z39.48-1984.

Library of Congress Cataloging-in-Publication Data

Scalise, Charles J.
    Hermeneutics as theological prolegomena : a canonical
approach / by Charles. J. Scalise.
    xiv + 155 pp.   6" x 9" (15 x 23
cm.)
    — (Studies in American biblical hermeneutics : 8)
    Includes bibliographical references and index.
    ISBN 1-86554-434-4 (hard).   — ISBN 0-86554-435-2 (pbk.)
    1. Bible—Hermeneutics. 2. Bible—Criticism, Canonical.
    3. Theology, Doctrinal. 4. Revelation. 5. Childs, Brevard S.
    I. Title. II. Series.
    BS476.S32 1993
    220.6'01—dc20   93-36657
                                               CIP

CONTENTS

To PJ

"Love—is anterior to Life—
Posterior—to Death—
Initial of Creation, and
The Exponent of Earth—"

Emily Dickinson, #917

EDITOR'S PREFACE

During these early years of the provenance of *Studies in American Biblical Hermeneutics,* the series has lived up to its promise of being ecumenical and inter-disciplinary in orientation. Now with this volume of Charles Scalise it has become "inter-theological" as well, for who would deny that historical-critical scholarship and evangelical theology form largely isolated communities of interpretation on the American landscape?

This volume breaks new ground for the StABH series in several ways. Certainly it represents the first voice that explicitly assumes an evangelical orientation. Do not be misread into assuming that evangelical Christians are intended as the sole audience of this book, although their basic way of viewing the world is decisive for Scalise's theological grammar. It has been the intention of StABH from the beginning to offer a common platform upon which American theologians and religious scholars alike could share their understanding of the Bible in a universal language available to all. Indeed, the establishment of such a universal language itself has been seen as an urgent need in our society and an integral part of the purpose of the series. Repeatedly, the need for this series has shown itself in the environment of American religious provincialism, i.e., limiting the scope of the book to one or another community of interpretation. The failure of religious thinkers to embrace fully the fabric of the American cultural context in the process of hammering out religious interpretation and meaning continues to have dire consequences for the vitality and relevance of our religious lives. The absence of the voice of the thoughtful evangelical in this series has unduly hampered our collective efforts to embrace more fully the "Americanness" of our theological experience. Now that omission can be put behind us with the hope that others will now feel more welcomed to enter the conversation.

Scalise establishes new territory for the series in another way by illustrating the desire among thoughtful evangelical theologians to enter the mainstream of critical thought in modern American life. As the author points out, it is erroneous to equate the terms "evangelical" and "pre-critical," although many assume such to be the case. This book crosses over from an exclusively evangelical orientation to the heart of post-critical hermeneutical thought. Scalise establishes his argument on the basis of a knowledgeable encounter with such post-critical thinkers as Søren Kierkegaard, Ludwig Wittgenstein, Hans-Georg Gadamer, Paul Ricoeur, and, especially, Brevard Childs. Scalise shows that it *is* possible to be evangelical *and* also knowingly engage primary concepts of representative post-critical thinkers. The specific direction that Scalise sketches out for us in this prolegomena to a post-critical evangelical theology is a nuanced form of Childs' canonical hermeneutical theory. Scalise's position is "nuanced" in the sense that he does not uncritically accept Childs' proposals concerning the priority of canon for biblical interpretation. Interestingly, however, his critique of Childs does not rest on *evangelical-critical* (a new category itself, perhaps, for main-stream scholars) grounds, but is made in a spirit analogous to historical-critical scholarship. While the canonical-critical thought of Childs is clearly *not* evangelical as such, it does have affinities to it in the sense of giving priority of meaning to the final form of biblical texts. It is not a large step from this position to one that emphasizes the doctrine of revelation as does evangelicalism. And, make no mistake about it, a preservation of the revelatory dimension of the Bible is something that evangelical thought in America has not given up on and continues to persist upon preserving. It remains to be seen whether, or in what sense, historical-critical theology will follow suit—and precisely what will be gained or lost as a result.

Scalise proposes an evangelical prologue to theology that is not opposed to the historical-critical methodologies that enjoy preeminence in the European academy and in main-stream American scholarship. It is the reductionistic utilization of these methodologies that he finds problematical. He argues that the heritage of the Enlightenment has resulted in an over-identification with history as the defining intellectual category that marks the contours of our theological thinking. As such, a post-critical evangelical biblical hermeneutic is not to be established on the basis of the denial of the foundational role of historical consciousness (that is the basis of criticism itself), but simply a more modest understanding of its role in the enterprise of theology. This means, above all, refusing to reduce the reality of God and the revelation of Scripture to categories of human thought and/or experience.

This evangelical position has a democratic flavor that is in keeping with American ideals and which has not always been maintained in historical-critical circles. Privileging God over humans is potentially the most democratic position, because when humans are privileged in general (as is the tendency of critical thought), is it not always *certain* humans that are privileged rather than *all*? An absolute dependence upon history implies an absolute relativism, and a dependence upon the professional scholar who alone can make historical context known to us. The post-critical evangelical territory that Scalise suggests to us is a self-consciously democratic one that places the experience of the faith community before the work of such human critical reflection. As he shows us, such a position need not be either naive not oppressive to those who do not share this presuppositional framework.

Finally, this book is the first in the series to address suggestively basic tenants of traditional Christian theology, especially the concepts of revelation, incarnation, and the Trinity. As noted, Scalise understands a post-critical evangelical canonical hermeneutics to be a prolegomena to Christian theology. He not only argues this formally, but suggests ways that this project might be fully carried out. By this very fact I believe that he is illustrating in this book the more important role Christian theology plays in evangelical circles than it does in main-stream historical criticism. Some, no doubt, would argue that this is all very much in favor of the latter. It seems to me that such a view is mistaken. The endlessly putting off of theology in historical-critical scholarship is hardly a sign of strength, but an idicator of a fundamental incapacity to do this work. In addition, the institutional division of our time between academy and church seems to have resulted in a kind of loss of nerve on the part of scholarship. All too frequently, the overthrow of dogma has resulted in a greatly diminished place for the things of faith, such as the humility of reason, the imperative of ethics, and the celebration of joyful community.

Reading this book will significantly enrich our understanding of how the Bible can be thoughtfully read by a major interpretive stream within American life. The book sketches out new terrain for evangelical theology, thereby becoming an enrichment for both historical-critical scholarship *and* evangelicalism.

Charles Mabee
Ecumenical Theological Center / Detroit
31 December 1993

FOREWORD

Christians facing the third millenium need to reenvision and renew their understandings of the relationship between Scripture and doctrine. The time-honored ways of describing the connections between the Bible and the teachings of Christian communities—whether by traditional or historical-critical means—are not adequate by themselves to meet the challenges of a postcritical age. The scholarly enterprise of Christian theology is in a confused state of ferment. Systematic approaches to Christian doctrine, which since the Enlightenment have relied heavily upon the idea of revelation to build a hermeneutical bridge between the "historical material" of Scripture and the "philosophical categories" of doctrine, are under serious attack.

Protestant evangelical communities that assume the primacy of Scripture as authority and norm for the development of doctrine are particularly threatened by the postcritical undermining of the foundations of the hermeneutical bridge. Older revelation-centered approaches that utilize a propositionalism based upon historical facts (e.g., Protestant fundamentalism) or a history of salvation model based upon the interpretation of historical events (e.g., the biblical theology movement) are vulnerable to criticisms of their philosophical foundations. Evangelical theology needs to discover new approaches to the interpretation of Scripture and its interface with Christian doctrine that will respond to the intellectual challenges of the present day.

This book offers one approach to guide evangelical theology in its movement from Scripture to Christian doctrine. Canonical hermeneutics provides this alternative route to revelation-centered categories. Specifically, a modified version of the canonical approach to biblical interpretation of Brevard S. Childs is formulated and then applied to the development of prolegomena to a postcritical evangelical theology.

The perspective of this work obviously reflects my own stance as an ecumenical, evangelical theologian in the Baptist tradition. The proposal is particularly directed to thoughtful evangelical Christians who, like myself, approach the theological task with the assumption of the authority of Scripture. From my teaching experiences in theological education, I have become convinced that there is quite a number of pastors, teachers, and other leaders in the broadly evangelical tradition who are both aware of contemporary intellectual culture and confessionally loyal to the authority of Scripture. The theology of the church should empower them to be able to love God with *all* of their mind, without sacrificing what they know of the truth through their education and culture.

I also hope that some aspects of this work will prove useful to the many other Christians who value the importance of the Bible in their understanding of the faith, even though they might not grant such a special place to its authority as Scripture. Although my argument is directed to those who assume the final authority of Scripture, all Christian communities that use the Bible to shape their Christian identity may find some benefit in careful theological reflection upon its functions as canon.

I am, of course, aware of many of the other routes Christians have taken on the way between the Bible and Christian doctrine —or even vice versa! A number of these other routes (e.g., mystical theology, Eastern Orthodox theology, liturgical theology) have much to teach evangelicals about the aesthetic depth and cross-cultural nature of the Christian faith. Each tradition that confesses Jesus as Lord has its own contribution to make to the people of God who comprise the church across time and culture. I pray that this theological appropriation of canonical hermeneutics will represent a faithful contribution to the church as it confronts the continuing challenge of understanding the relationship between Scripture and doctrine.

The writing of this book has entailed an extravagant debt of gratitude to so many colleagues and friends. The following lines acknowledge only some of the principal participants in the process.

The administration of the Southern Baptist Theological Seminary made study leave available, during which the research and writing of the first three chapters was largely accomplished. The Education Commission of the Southern Baptist Convention provided support for the project through the M. May Robertson-J.W. Farmer Scholarship/Loan Program.

Paul S. Fiddes, Principal of Regent's Park College, Oxford, offered the opportunity to become a member of the Senior Common Room of the College, as well as hosting some lively occasions for collegial dialogue regarding my research and our mutual theological interests. Dean Larry Kreitzer not only engaged me in some stimulating discussions regarding biblical hermeneutics, but also shared the gift of caring friendship. I am also grateful to the many other members of the Senior Common Room who expressed interest in the progress of my research.

G. Ernest Nicholson, Provost of Oriel College, and Mrs. Hazel Nicholson took our family under their wing and provided us with spacious housing accomodation and gracious Oxford hospitality.

My *Doktorvater*, William L. Hendricks, guided my interest in hermeneutics during my years of graduate study and supervised my dissertation, which laid essential groundwork for the research of the present study.

Karen E. Smith, now at the University of Cardiff, and Amy Plantinga Pauw of Louisville Presbyterian Theological Seminary kindly read parts of this work and furnished constructive criticism that resulted in a number of improvements. Dan R. Stiver of Southern Seminary patiently read the entire manuscript chapter by chapter and offered the gentle but thorough critique which has led to significant reformulation and clearer communication of the vision that underlies this project. Of course, all responsibility for the murkiness that remains is my own, but thanks to these colleagues there are fewer "dark corners" in this book.

Cecil P. Staton, Jr. of Mercer University Press supplied encouragement during the final stages of the writing, while managing editor Scott Nash skillfully guided the actual publishing process. Charles Mabee, the series editor, furnished thoughtful review and suggested some helpful additional resources.

Pamela Scalise, my beloved partner in life and work, has graced my life with that committed daily companionship of mind and heart that sustained this work from its earliest imaginings to its final form. David and Daniel, our two lively sons, gave salutary reminders that a canonical reading is certainly not the only way to understand the Holy Bible.

Charles J. Scalise
Louisville, Kentucky
September 1993

THE CRISIS: REVELATION
AS THEOLOGICAL PROLEGOMENA

The declaration that Christian theology is in crisis has become a commonplace in our pluralistic age.[1] Multiple paradigms compete unsuccessfully for widespread consensus in the field. When one confronts this "shattered spectrum" of late twentieth-century theology, bewilderment—rather than mere confusion—seems the order of the day.[2] One wonders how scholarly theological construction ever became entangled in such complex and often faddish linguistic thickets. Scholars from similar religious communities and traditions commonly talk past one another.[3] Eminent theologians frequently use the same terms (e.g., salvation, church) to point to radically different referents.[4]

· The Theologian's Dilemma: Disorder in the Garden ·

The Christian theologian who seeks to engage in constructive theological reflection finds himself or herself in a real dilemma. Jean-Pierre Torrell strikingly portrays the contemporary situation:

---

[1]The decades-long existence of a popular theological magazine entitled *Christianity and Crisis* is a contemporary cultural token illustrating this situation.

[2]This vivid image describing the current theological crisis is used by Lonnie D. Kliever, *The Shattered Spectrum: A Survey of Contemporary Theology* (Richmond: John Knox Press, 1981).

[3]For example, William Placher candidly admits, "I have therefore found it unnerving to read critics of postliberal theology [Placher's own position] denouncing it for its indifference to philosophy and indeed to modern culture generally. I wondered if we were reading the same theological texts. I wondered, frankly, what philosophy they had been reading" (William C. Placher, *Unapologetic Theology: A Christian Voice in a Pluralistic Conversation* [Louisville KY: Westminster/John Knox Press, 1989] 7).

[4]The Barth-Tillich or the Barth-Bultmann debates are commonly used to introduce beginning students of twentieth-century theology to this phenomenon. A more revealing comparison is offered by Robert Clyde Johnson, who distinguishes five different uses for the term "revelation" underneath the umbrella of dialectical theology (Unpublished lectures on Christian Doctrine, Yale University Divinity School, 1975).

This picture [Torrell's description of fundamental theology] resembles a French garden in that it points out avenues through a reality which would otherwise be pretty much an expanse of matted underbrush. As a matter of fact, the picture only partially represents the reality which, taken in its full dimensions, is much less orderly.[5]

How does one develop a theology that is faithful to both the Scriptures and the Christian community, yet honestly takes into account the lack of consensus in postcritical scholarship?[6] How does a contemporary evangelical theologian—a Christian thinker who begins with the assumption of the primacy of Scripture[7]—move from the Bible to doctrine in a fashion that makes sense to Christians who live amidst the clamor of pluralistic postmodernity?[8]

This book represents one preliminary attempt to respond to these questions. It attempts to negotiate the hazardous divide between Scripture and doctrine. Since the time of the Enlightenment, thoughtful Christians have experienced increasing difficulty

---

[5]Jean-Pierre Torrell, "New Trends in Fundamental Theology in the Postconciliar Period," in René Latourelle and Gerald O'Collins (eds.), *Problems and Perspectives in Fundamental Theology*, trans. Matthew J. O'Connell (New York: Paulist Press, 1982) 11-22, at 14.

[6]By "postcritical scholarship" I am referring to the great variety of competing methods and paradigms that seek to shape scholarship in religion and the humanities following the decline of the historical-critical paradigm as the sole dominant model of academic scholarship. For further discussion and examples, see the sections dealing with "The Formal Problem" and "The Material Problem" later in this chapter. In the section entitled "A Modest Proposal" I will further explain the postcritical nature of my own approach.

[7]For further explanation of this working definition of the Protestant "evangelical" perspective, see the following discussion on the assumption of the centrality of Scripture. Later in this chapter, at the beginning of the section entitled "A Modest Proposal: Canonical Hermeneutics and Theological Prolegomena," I seek to locate myself within this tradition.

[8]Diogenes Allen offers a helpful introduction to the issues in the discussion between Christianity and postmodernity in *Christian Belief in a Postmodern World: The Full Wealth of Conviction* (Louisville KY: Westminster/John Knox Press, 1989). See especially the Introduction, "The End of the Modern World: A New Openness for Faith" (1-19) and the references cited there (217-18).

in demonstrating the continuity between the language of Scripture and the proposals of Christian doctrine that claim to be authorized by Scripture.[9] I am seeking to develop one approach to the articulation of a biblically-grounded theology. I hope that this project will be of value to thoughtful Christians who assume that the Scriptures should be the primary "point of departure" and evaluative norm for the formulation of doctrine.[10]

The centrality of Scripture in the theological enterprise will *not* be the focus of argument in this volume. Rather the argument will assume that Scripture, rather than either church tradition or religious experience, is the "norm-making norm" (*norma normans*) for Christian doctrine.[11] Of course, this view does not imply that tradition and experience are unimportant sources of religious authority for the Christian community. The claim is rather that primary mediated authority (i.e., authority under God in Christ) rests with the interpretation of Scripture.

One way of describing this claim of the primary mediated authority of Scripture is in response to the following question: If the risen Christ has received "all authority in heaven and on earth" from God (Matt 28:18), then how is this authority transmitted to the church today? In an evangelical view, Scripture, preserved and interpreted by the Christian community and actualized in personal religious experience, is the primary means in which the authority of God in Christ is mediated to Christians today. The centrality of Scripture for the formulation of Christian

---

[9]David Kelsey has offered an incisive analysis of the various ways modern theologians—both liberal and conservative—have used Scripture to authorize their theological proposals in *The Uses of Scripture in Recent Theology* (Philadelphia: Fortress Press, 1975).

[10]I am here indebted to Søren Kierkegaard's reflections on the need for an "historical point of departure for an eternal consciousness" in *Philosophical Fragments or A Fragment of Philosophy*, 2d ed., trans. David Swenson and Howard Hong (Princeton: Princeton University Press, 1962); see especially Kierkegaard's three questions on the title page.

[11]For a useful survey of contemporary theological options on the question of authority, see Gabriel Fackre, *The Christian Story: A Pastoral Systematics*, vol. 2, *Authority: Scripture in the Church for the World* (Grand Rapids: Eerdmans, 1987) 60-156. Fackre's perspective is that of an "ecumenical evangelical."

doctrine functions as a "background belief," thus playing a constitutive role in this theological perspective.[12]

Before offering an initial statement of the proposal of this work, it is necessary first to explore briefly the historical background and the formal and material problems to which the argument responds. The following three sections of this chapter are devoted to these tasks.

· The Historical Background: Modern Theology and the Doctrine of Revelation ·

Christian theology from its inception has either included or assumed a doctrine of revelation—an account or implicit set of beliefs concerning how God has revealed Godself to humanity.[13] Until the time of the Enlightenment, however, the doctrine of revelation was a secondary or peripheral doctrine.[14] Christian theologians generally *assumed* that God was knowable by humanity as

---

[12]Ronald Thiemann offers the following explanation of the term "background belief": "Every coherent system of belief rests upon certain convictions which are assumed to be true and thus provide stability for the whole framework. These beliefs are *basic* because the coherence of many other beliefs depends upon the acceptance of these beliefs as true, and they are *background* because their axiomatic status makes explicit justification of them unnecessary. While these background beliefs are not immune to revision, they must remain relatively fixed in order for the framework to remain stable" (Ronald F. Thiemann, *Revelation and Theology: The Gospel as Narrated Promise* [Notre Dame: Univ. of Notre Dame Press, 1985] 11). For bibliography related to the philosophical development and theological elaboration of this notion, see Thiemann, 160, n. 7.

[13]Avery Dulles offers a useful introductory account of the historical development of the doctrine of revelation in *Revelation Theology: A History* (New York: Herder and Herder, 1969). Dulles is dependent upon the work of René Latourelle, *Théologie de la Révélation*, 2d ed. (Bruges: Desclée de Brouwer, 1966). An English translation, published in 1966 by Alba House in Staten Island NY, was not available to me. More recently Dulles has written *Models of Revelation* (Dublin: Gill and Macmillan, 1983), which provides much helpful description and categorization of diverse views, as well as an attempt at systematic restatement.

[14]Dulles (*Models of Revelation*, ix, 4, 12, 20, and 36) points to the role of seventeenth century controversies with the Deists in shaping the development of the doctrine.

a gift of God's grace, except for problems due to the blindness of sin.[15] The assumption that God was in principle knowable was seen as self-evident—a background belief held by most educated persons in the cultures where Christianity (and Judaism and Islam) were dominant. The principal questions that theology had to answer were "How can I know God?" and "How can I be saved?" —not "Is God knowable?" and "What evidence do you have for your claims?"

René Descartes, "the Father of the Enlightenment," began the shift to the Enlightenment ideal of knowledge with his *Meditations on First Philosophy*, written in 1639–1640.[16] Descartes urged his readers to test everything they believed by systematically submitting it to doubt. In fact, *dubito ergo sum* ('I doubt, therefore I am') may be a more accurate description for Descartes' method than his famous motto *cogito ergo sum* ('I think, therefore I am'). Descartes maintained that such a process would provide a sure foundation for knowledge.[17]

Then in the latter eighteenth century Immanuel Kant shattered the background belief that God is in principle knowable. In his *Critique of Pure Reason* Kant demonstrated that we can only know things as we perceive them to be (phenomena), not as they are in themselves.[18] "Transtemporal realities" cannot be directly known.[19]

---

[15]For a description of this assumption in the theology of John Calvin, see Thiemann, *Revelation and Theology*, 11. Thiemann states, "The reformers did not attempt to demonstrate that the knowledge of God is a gift of God's grace; they simply assumed that it was the case" (ibid.)

[16]René Descartes, *Discourse on Method and the Meditations*, trans. F. E. Sutcliffe (Harmondsworth: Penguin Books, 1968).

[17]For further discussion of Descartes' role in the beginnings of Enlightenment foundationalism see Placher, *Unapologetic Theology*, 24-26, 29, and 35. For a discussion of Descartes' impact upon the status of the doctrine of revelation see Thiemann, *Revelation and Theology*, 12-14.

[18]Immanuel Kant, *Critique of Pure Reason*, trans. J. M. D. Meiklejohn (London: George Bell and Sons, 1901), "Transcendental Doctrine of the Faculty of Judgment," chap. 3, "The ground of division of all objects into Phenomena and Noumena." For a detailed introductory exposition of Kant's views, see Frederick Copleston, *A History of Philosophy*, vol. 6, pt. 2 (Garden City NY: Doubleday [Image], 1964), especially chaps. 11 and 13.

Kant's challenge shook the foundations of traditional theology. The primary question for modern theology (i.e., theology that takes Kant's epistemological analysis and its critique of revelation seriously[20]) shifted from "how does one know God?" to "is God knowable at all?"—or more popularly, from "how do you get saved?" to "what do you have to go on?"[21] As a result of this shift, since the Enlightenment the doctrine of revelation has been the centerpiece of modern theological prolegomena.

The doctrine of revelation has been elevated from a secondary and peripheral doctrine to the first and most elaborately argued doctrine.[22] Theologians—both "liberals" and "conservatives"—have sought to use the doctrine of revelation to provide the foundation for all of their doctrinal assertions. From the Enlightenment until the middle of the twentieth century the degree of historical consensus on this approach to modern theology was truly amazing. In the words of the stalwart Princeton conservative B. B. Warfield,

> Most types of modern theology explicitly allow that all knowledge of God rests on revelation. . . . In this the extremest "liberals" . . . agree with the extremest "conservatives."[23]

---

[19]For Kant's demonstration of the impossibility of proving the existence of God, see "Transcendental Dialectic," book 2, chap. 3, "The Ideal of Pure Reason," especially sections 3-7.

[20]An example of the centrality of Kant's critique in nineteenth century disputes over revelation may be found in F. D. Maurice's detailed polemic against Mansel's Bampton lectures (F. D. Maurice, *What is Revelation?* [Cambridge: Macmillan, 1859], especially 150-53, 376-79, and 395-98).

[21]As P. T. Forsyth observed at the beginning of this century, "The principle of authority is ultimately the whole religious question" (*The Principle of Authority in Relation to Certainty, Sanctity and Society: An Essay in the Philosophy of Experimental Religion* [London: Hodder and Stoughton, 1912] 3).

[22]Even a cursory survey of post-Enlightenment Western theologies will substantiate this assertion. The first two volumes of Karl Barth's *Church Dogmatics* perhaps provide the most dramatic example of this development.

[23]Benjamin Breckinridge Warfield, "The Idea of Revelation and Theories of Revelation," in *Revelation and Inspiration* (New York: Oxford University Press, 1927) 37-48, at 37.

As a result of this method, every conceivable (and sometimes inconceivable) challenge to Christian doctrine both from within and without the Christian church is wrestled with *before* the doctrine of God—the One who is purportedly being revealed—is expounded. One could perhaps even argue the following case only half-facetiously: the *physical length* of revelation-centered theological prolegomena in modern systematic theologies has increased in proportion to the increasing epistemological complications of the centuries since the Enlightenment! Concern with theological method has overshadowed concern with the theological content of doctrine. At times it seems as if contemporary theologians are so mired in the epistemological morass of revelation-centered prolegomena that they never will be able to get onto the tasks of doctrinal reflection and reformulation.[24]

· The Formal Problem: The Crisis of Revelation-Centered Prolegomena ·

A number of Christian theologians have argued for more than a quarter century that the theological elevation of the doctrine of revelation is in serious trouble.[25] This critique raises the "formal problem" of how theology is ordered or organized, rather than discussing the content of theology. The "rules of the game" of theology are what is at stake.

Perhaps the most dramatic polemic has come from F. Gerald Downing, who denies any value to the doctrine at all.[26] One need

---

[24]The theological writings of David Tracy offer one contemporary example of this pattern. As William Placher admits, "A good many people—myself included—have urged contemporary theologians to abandon their preoccupation with methodology and get on with the business of really doing theology. I therefore confess embarrassment at being the author of a sort of extended preface to contemporary discussions about theological method" (*Unapologetic Theology*, 7). As the writer of this book on prolegomena, I must hastily add my own *mea culpa* to that of Placher.

[25]For an overview of some of the most important of these charges, see Thiemann, *Revelation and Theology*, 1-7 and 157-59.

[26]F. Gerald Downing, *Has Christianity A Revelation?* (Philadelphia: Westminster Press, 1964).

not endorse Downing's attack upon the doctrine itself in order to agree with his assertion that, "The word 'revelation' is a source of great confusion. A theology based on it is inadequate for the exposition of the traditional faith of Christians."[27]

The Enlightenment-initiated shift of the doctrine of revelation from a secondary doctrine articulating a background belief held by most educated persons in Western culture to the foundational belief for all Christian theology has been under attack on at least three major fronts.

The first front is exegetical. The use of the idea of "revelation" as an umbrella concept to describe all of God's dealings with humanity has doubtful biblical warrant.[28] James Barr has demonstrated that such a broad use of the term does not do justice to the wide diversity of ways in which the Bible portrays God's interaction with humanity, nor to the specific ways in which the Bible uses the notion of revelation.[29] Barr summarizes his critique as follows:

> My argument is not against the word "revelation," but against the way in which the use of this word has grouped together a number of different things and so distorts them. . . . In the Bible, however, the usage of the terms which roughly correspond to "revelation" is both limited and specialized.[30]

In short, theology centered upon the doctrine of revelation is biblically inadequate.

The second front of attack is philosophical. Widespread suspicion of foundationalism of any sort characterizes contemporary philosophy.[31] In particular, the epistemological foundationalism upon which modern theologians have relied in their theories of

---

[27]Ibid., 274.

[28]John Baillie's *The Idea of Revelation in Recent Thought* (New York: Columbia University Press, 1956) offers a classic introductory exposition of this approach.

[29]James Barr, *Old and New in Interpretation: A Study of the Two Testaments* (London: SCM Press, 1966) 65-102, especially 82ff. See also Barr's later work, *The Bible in the Modern World* (London: SCM Press, 1973), 112-32, especially 120ff.

[30]Barr, *Old and New in Interpretation*, 86, 88.

[31]See Placher, *Unapologetic Theology*, especially 24-54.

revelation is vulnerable, since it depends upon a special category of "intuition." As Thiemann contends,

> The fatal flaw which haunts the modern doctrine of revelation . . . is the epistemological foundationalism which theologians employ in order to provide the theoretical justification for Christian belief in God's prevenience. This foundationalism, which relies on an incoherent notion of non-inferential intuition as the means of asserting the priority of God's gracious reality, can be seen in theologians as diverse as John Locke, Friedrich Schleiermacher, and Thomas Torrance.[32]

Whether or not Thiemann succeeds in showing the logical "incoherence" of post-Enlightenment doctrines of revelation, he certainly points to a weakness of these approaches, which renders questionable the method of elevating revelation to the status of the primary doctrine upon which all others rest.

The third front on which the elevation of the doctrine of revelation has been challenged is pastoral. The shift of focus of Christian theology from the Reformation's emphasis upon grace and faith to the Enlightenment's emphasis upon reason and evidence has distracted both theologians and laity from the central themes of the faith. Questions of apologetical evidence overshadow questions of saving grace. One may get a sense for the impact of this shift by comparing Luther's 1535 commentary on Galatians[33] with John Locke's *The Reasonableness of Christianity*.[34]

At a popular level the success of works like Josh McDowell's *Evidence that Demands a Verdict* points to the distortions wrought by the debased triumph of the Enlightenment evidentialist approach to Christian theology.[35] Coming to faith has been reduced

---

[32]Thiemann, *Revelation and Theology*, 7. For Thiemann's development of this thesis, see 9-46.

[33]Martin Luther, *Lectures on Galatians*, vol. 26 of *Luther's Works*, ed. Jaroslav Pelikan (St. Louis: Concordia, 1963).

[34]John Locke, *The Reasonableness of Christianity with A Discourse of Miracles and Part of A Third Letter Concerning Toleration*, ed. I. T. Ramsey (London: Adam and Charles Black, 1958).

[35]Josh McDowell, *Evidence That Demands A Verdict* (San Bernardino CA: Campus Crusade for Christ [Here's Life Publishers], 1972) and also *More Evidence that Demands a Verdict* (San Bernardino CA: Campus Crusade for Christ [Here's

to changing one's mind based upon assent to piles of "factual evidence." The love of God becomes lost in the quest for "facts" that purportedly compel faith.

The attacks upon the doctrine of revelation on biblical, philosophical, and pastoral grounds have found their mark. The elevation of revelation to the status of the foundational doctrine upon which all of the rest of Christian theology stands or falls is now in serious question. Is a revelation-centered approach to Christian doctrine still intellectually viable? If so, does it remain the best approach to systematic theological reflection in our time?[36]

Along with these attacks upon the increasing importance of the doctrine of revelation, contemporary biblical scholarship has witnessed widespread questioning of the utility of the historical-critical paradigm that has dominated academic biblical study. So, before considering a differing approach to the formal issue of the location of the doctrine of revelation, we need to examine the material problem posed for systematic theology by the declining hegemony of the historical-critical method of biblical interpretation.

· The Material Problem: The Decline of the Historical-Critical Paradigm ·

The rise of critical historical study following the Enlightenment posed a serious challenge for Protestant Christians who advocated the primacy of Scripture.[37] The application of historical-critical methods to the text of the Bible—especially to the Gospels—challenged the validity of Christian doctrines that claimed to be

---

Life Publishers], 1975). The republication of both of these volumes in Britain in 1990 provides further indication of the continuing consequences of the popular expression of revelation-centered theology.

[36]The term "systematic" is used here to refer to any form of theology that seeks to offer an ordered, comprehensive account of Christian belief according to some doctrinal or conceptual scheme. The use of the classical Lombardian ordering or some modification of it, while historically significant, is not intended in my use of the term.

[37]For a detailed chronicling of the exegetical and hermeneutical dimensions of this challenge, see Hans Frei, *The Eclipse of Biblical Narrative: A Study in Eighteenth and Nineteenth Century Hermeneutics* (New Haven CT: Yale University Press, 1974).

based upon the historical truth of the Scriptures.[38] As Albert Schweitzer pictures the problem, "Modern historical theology, therefore, with its three-quarters scepticism, is left at last with only a torn and tattered Gospel of Mark in its hands."[39]

Various apologetic strategies were attempted in response to this crisis. Some theologians—following Friedrich Schleiermacher[40] —shifted the focus of authority from Scripture to religious experience. Many biblical exegetes and theologians, however, developed elaborate apologetic approaches that sought to locate the truth of faith (revelation) in the history ("events") that occurred *behind* the texts of the Scripture.[41] The Bible formally preserves its authority, but its relation to revelation changes. Instead of the texts themselves being directly revelatory, the texts *witness* to the truth of revelation occurring in history.

The Christian believer who takes biblical scholarship seriously is therefore left in an uneasy and unstable dependence upon the contingencies of historical-critical research for the biblical warrants of his or her faith.[42] Any number of concrete illustrations of this situation could be chosen. To present a rather uncomplicated

---

[38]The classic description and critique of this process is Albert Schweitzer's *The Quest of the Historical Jesus: A Critical Study of Its Progress from Reimarus to Wrede*, 3d ed., trans. W. Montgomery (London: Adam and Charles Black, 1954).

[39]Ibid., 307.

[40]Friedrich Schleiermacher, *The Christian Faith*, ed. H. R. Mackintosh and J. S. Stewart, 2 vols. (New York: Harper and Row, 1963). Frei offers a perceptive description of the hermeneutical "sea change" wrought by Schleiermacher (*Eclipse*, 282-306). For an insightful analysis of the relevance of Schleiermacher's approach for contemporary theology, see Stephen Sykes, *The Identity of Christianity: Theologians and the Essence of Christianity* (London: S.P.C.K., 1984), 81-101, 297-300, and *passim*.

[41]The German *Heilsgeschichtlicheschule* and the American "biblical theology" movement offer twentieth-century examples of this approach. For a detailed analysis of the latter movement see Brevard S. Childs, *Biblical Theology in Crisis* (Philadelphia: Westminster Press, 1970).

[42]Søren Kierkegaard depicts the inadequacies of this situation in *Philosophical Fragments*, chap. 5, "The Disciple at Second Hand," especially 126.

exegetical example, which reflects the consensus of much current critical scholarship, I turn to the book of Amos.[43]

Historical-critical research concludes that the prophet Amos did not write all of the oracles contained in the biblical book that bears his name. Specifically, the historical Amos (i.e., the figure of Amos reconstructed by the methods of historical-critical research) only spoke the oracles of judgement in the book and not the oracles of salvation found in the last chapter (Amos 9:11-15). In the words of James Luther Mays,

> The oracles of salvation at the end of the book (9.11-15) presuppose a different time and situation from that of Amos, probably the exilic period.[44]

Commenting on 9:12, Mays flatly declares, "This promise of salvation is hardly a saying of Amos."[45]

Therefore, the last oracle of the book of Amos is labeled "secondary" and is viewed as being of only peripheral worth in reconstructing the message of the book. Instead of the precritical interpretation of Amos, which pictures a prophet who proclaims both the reality of God's judgement and the promise of God's salvation, believing Jews and Christians who take biblical scholarship seriously are left with only an Amos of "gloom and doom." The dilemma for thoughtful Christians is not unlike that posed by Schweitzer's image of "a torn and tattered Gospel of Mark." The contingent reconstructions of historical-critical scholarship lead to a theological attenuation of the message of the book of Amos,

---

[43]While specialists might, of course, disagree with my assumption of significant consensus here, such disagreement in itself would provide another illustration of the contingencies of historical-critical research and the dilemma this situation poses for biblical warrants of faith.

[44]James Luther Mays, *Amos: A Commentary* (Philadelphia: Westminster, 1969) 13. For further analysis of the historical-critical discussion of Amos 9 since Wellhausen, see Brevard S. Childs, *Introduction to the Old Testament as Scripture* (Philadelphia: Fortress Press, 1979; also London: SCM Press, 1979), 405-10. This book will hereafter be referred to as Childs, *IOTS*.

[45]Ibid., 165.

instead of an enrichment of it. As the Catholic historian, Ignace de la Potterie, observes,

> The critical historical method is necessarily limited and reductive. It plays a legitimate and even necessary role, provided it recognizes its limitations, but it becomes unacceptable when it claims to be the sole method and seeks to be applied in every possible area, or when it condemns every other approach, for example, that of faith.[46]

Moreover, recent decades have witnessed a proliferation of new literary-critical, sociological, and other (e.g., feminist, materialist, liberationist) approaches to biblical interpretation that have challenged the hegemony of the historical-critical paradigm.[47] Although Gerhard Maier's proclamation of *The End of the Historical-Critical Method* is overdrawn, the days when the historical-critical paradigm dominated the whole field of biblical scholarship are at an end.[48] The existence of competing paradigms for biblical interpretation—none of which can claim to control the field—adds an additional dimension to the material problem of revelation-centered prolegomena.

Our brief survey of the historical background and the formal and material problems associated with the use of revelation as the central theme of theological prolegomena underscores again the dilemma facing contemporary evangelical theology. Given this closer inspection of the nature of the "disorder in the garden," we are now prepared to examine an initial statement of the proposal this book explores.

---

[46]Ignace de la Potterie, "History and Truth," in René Latourelle and Gerald O'Collins (eds)., *Problems and Perspectives of Fundamental Theology*, trans. Matthew O'Connell (New York: Paulist Press, 1982) 87-104, at 92.

[47]For a useful introductory survey of many of these approaches in the field of Old Testament, see John Barton, *Reading the Old Testament: Method in Biblical Study* (London: Darton, Longman, and Todd, 1984). A useful example of the application of a variety of new literary critical approaches to New Testament interpretation is R. Alan Culpepper, *Anatomy of the Fourth Gospel: A Study of Literary Design* (Philadelphia: Fortress Press, 1983).

[48]Gerhaed Maier, *The End of the Historical method*, trans. E. W. Leverenz and R. F. Norden (St. Louis: Concordia, 1977).

· A Modest Proposal:
Canonical Hermeneutics and Theological Prolegomena ·

The argument of this book is a modest one. Having experienced in a pluralist culture the vulnerability of approaches that seek to make universal truth claims based on dubious philosophical and historiographical foundations, I am offering an hypothesis that claims a more limited range of applicability.[49]

I am espousing a hermeneutical view of the language of Christian theology that understands theological statements as "insider's language"—language based upon the living traditions of the Jewish and Christian communities.[50] The perspective from which I speak may be labeled "broadly evangelical," while my particular denominational family is Baptist. By the label "broadly evangelical," I denote my assumption of the primacy of Scripture described above.[51] Also, this label implies that I am claiming that my arguments are directly applicable to those communities of Christians that share my perspective that the Scriptures provide the primary point of departure and evaluative norm for the formulation of Christian doctrine. I hope that others who do not share my broadly evangelical perspective but value the importance of the Bible in the Christian faith will find some of the proposals of this study interesting and perhaps even useful in their own theologies. I am not, however, claiming that my argument applies directly to them, nor *a fortiori* to the many others who claim a Christian identity but question whether Scripture has any positive role to play in the continuing shaping of their communities.

---

[49]Of course, I am not here disavowing any truth claims that the Scriptures make for the Christian faith. I am simply avoiding the dubious arguments others have made (often naively or dogmatically claiming the authority of Scripture) for their interpretations of the faith. For a helpful analysis of the situation in regard to the Bible and theological assertions, see Kelsey, *The Uses of Scripture in Recent Theology.*

[50]The second chapter of this book will develop this hermeneutical understanding of the language of theology in further detail.

[51]See the earlier section of this chapter entitled "The Theologian's Dilemma."

Given these limitations, my modest proposal may be stated as follows: *A carefully nuanced understanding of canonical hermeneutics can serve as the central theme of prolegomena to a postcritical evangelical theology.*

The word "postcritical" here refers not only to the general situation of much contemporary theological reflection, but specifically to the critique of the doctrine of revelation as the central category for theological prolegomena—"the formal problem" described above. Moreover, given the claim (not always true in fact) that evangelical theology takes critical biblical scholarship seriously, then the situation described above as "the material problem" points to the need for a new approach to the complex interface between Scripture and theology.

The term "canonical hermeneutics" refers to a modified version of the canonical approach to biblical interpretation developed by Brevard S. Childs.[52] Childs' proposal was first articulated in his *Introduction to the Old Testament as Scripture*.[53] Childs subsequently extended his approach in *The New Testament as Canon: An Introduction*.[54] He has pursued some application to the field of biblical theology in *Old Testament Theology in a Canonical Context*.[55] I am making some modifications to Childs' approach, which represent both a response to some justified criticism and an effort to make the approach more useful for doctrinal construction in a postcritical evangelical theology. This approach to canonical hermeneutics seeks to move beyond the task of reconstructing the history behind the text. It attempts to recapture the wider history of the use of the Bible as Scripture by faith communities, while not presupposing an elaborately grounded doctrine of revelation.

---

[52]The third chapter introduces Childs' approach and discusses the proposed modifications in detail.

[53]Childs, *IOTS*.

[54]Philadelphia: Fortress Press, 1985; also London: SCM Press, 1985, hereafter referred to as Childs, *NTAC*.

[55]Philadelphia: Fortress Press, 1986; also London: SCM Press, 1986, hereafter referred to as Childs, *OTT*. Unfortunately, Childs' newest work in this area, *Biblical Theology of the Old and New Testaments: Theological Reflection on the Christian Bible* (Philadelphia: Fortress Press, 1993), arrived after my research for this study was completed.

· A Brief Overview: The Plan of the Book ·

The remainder of this book is devoted to the exploration, development, and defense of my argument that canonical hermeneutics can provide broadly evangelical Christian communities with one useful approach for responding to the contemporary theological situation.

The second chapter examines some philosophical approaches that describe the nature and tasks of theological language. I contend that a cross-disciplinary theological hermeneutics can describe the categories of a new postcritical paradigm for evangelical theology. Such a theological hermeneutics is characterized by the integration of biblical, historical, literary, and philosophical perspectives into a dynamic model of levels of meaning.

The third chapter describes Childs' canonical approach to biblical interpretation. I engage a number of the significant criticisms made regarding Childs' work and propose several modifications, with the intention of enhancing his approach for the task of theological prolegomena.

The fourth chapter shows how this carefully nuanced understanding of canonical hermeneutics can become the central theme of postcritical prolegomena to an evangelical theology, which maintains legitimate continuity with both critical and precritical traditions.

The final chapter explores the application of this understanding of canonical hermeneutics to Christian doctrine. Particular attention is given to the development of a postcritical, canonical model of doctrinal exposition. The model includes some constructive reflection upon the implications of canonical hermeneutics for the shape of the doctrine of God.

THE CATEGORIES: CROSS-DISCIPLINARY THEOLOGICAL HERMENEUTICS

Underlying the crisis in revelation-centered prolegomena, which we examined in chapter one, is a contemporary philosophical problematic regarding the nature and tasks of theological language.[1] What is the status of the language that theologians use to describe God and God's works and ways in the world? What does it mean to talk about God in the language of theology?

In the twentieth century these issues have been hotly debated in both philosophical and theological circles, particularly in light of the so-called "turn to language" in contemporary philosophy. The purpose of this chapter, however, is not to survey the discussion[2] but to examine some themes arising from it that shape the ways in which canonical hermeneutics can function as theological prolegomena.[3] Specifically, I am arguing that a cross-disciplinary theological hermeneutics can structure the categories (or provide the philosophical "rules of the game") according to which evangelical theology can move from Scripture to doctrine.

Christian theologians have, of course, been concerned for millennia with philosophy of language and its relationship to the claims of Christian doctrine. A survey of this theme in the history

---

[1]Philosophical issues regarding the nature and task of theological language are, of course, part of the larger study of the nature of religious language, which in turn is a sub-field of the philosophy of language. For non-technical introductions to this field for theologically-inclined students, see Ian T. Ramsey, *Religious Language* (London: SCM Press, 1957) and Frederick Ferré, *Language, Logic, and God* (London: Eyre and Spottiswood, 1962). Peter Donovan's *Religious Language* (New York: Hawthorn Books, 1976) and Terence Tilley's *Talking of God: An Introduction to Philosophical Analysis of Religious Language* (New York: Paulist Press, 1978) also offer valuable introductions.

[2]My colleague Dan Stiver is in the process of preparing a textbook on religious language that will offer an updated introductory survey of these issues.

[3]I am not a professional philosopher and make no claim to specialization in the complex field of linguistic philosophy. Rather, my interest in these matters consists in their relationship to the claims that Christians make for language about God.

of doctrine would begin in earnest with the Greek apologists of the second century and reserve a special place for the recovery of Aristotle by Thomas Aquinas and others in the high Middle Ages. What is significant, however, about this theme in our time is the widespread rejection of the *categories* of classical metaphysics within which the issues have traditionally been joined. Not only the content, but the status of the classical language relating God and being (ontology) has been rendered dubious. We will begin with a brief examination of some of the criticisms of the theological use of the categories of classical metaphysics.

· The Critique of Classical Metaphysical Categories ·

At the heart of Christian theology's appropriation of the language of classical metaphysics has been a linkage of Being and God.[4] This linkage may be implicit or explicit, formally analogical[5] or nuanced in a host of ways.[6] In any case, the doctrine of God is tied in some fashion to philosophical ontology. Philosophy provides the general categories for talking about "what is," and then theology either adopts or modifies these categories to talk about the "God Who Is" (or, in our dynamic, future-oriented culture, the "God Who Becomes").[7]

---

[4]Similarly in the "neo-classical" metaphysics of process theology the linkage is between God and "Becoming." For a useful comparison between the doctrines of God in contemporary process theology (Ogden) and eschatological theology (Moltmann), see John J. O'Donnell, *Trinity and Temporality: The Christian Doctrine of God in the Light of Process Theology and the Theology of Hope* (Oxford: Oxford Univ. Press, 1983).

[5]In the history of Christian doctrine, for example, one may trace the history of the *analogia entis* ("analogy of being") in a variety of Christian Neoplatonic and Thomist theologies.

[6]For some sophisticated examples of the nuancing of this linkage between God and being in twentieth-century theology, see Paul Tillich, *Systematic Theology*, 3 vols. in 1 (Chicago: University of Chicago Press, 1968) and John Macquarrie, *Principles of Christian Theology*, rev. ed. (London: SCM Press, 1977).

[7]Perhaps the most explicit example is E. L. Mascall's *He Who Is: A Study in Traditional Theism* (London: Longmans, Green and Co., 1945).

Reshaped by the Enlightenment, this linkage between God and being became vastly more complicated through an emphasis upon the perspective of the knowing subject (Descartes' "I think, therefore I am"). Theology found itself entangled in a mesh of epistemological issues, which made the linkage between God and being increasingly problematic. If we cannot really know what "things in themselves" (Kant) are, then how can we claim to know (even analogically) the God who is?

Perhaps the most dramatic example of these epistemological complications to ontology may be found in the philosophy of Hegel, whose shadow dominated much of nineteenth- and early twentieth-century Protestant theology. Even a surface exploration of his complex system of thought, as expounded for instance in his monumental *The Phenomenology of Mind*, will convince aspiring metaphysical theologians that the linkage of God and being in terms of thought has become an enormously complex and difficult enterprise.[8]

Given this state of affairs, serious criticisms of metaphysical philosophy and its alliance with Cartesian theology emerged from a wide variety of perspectives (e.g., the economic materialism of Marx, the analytic psychology of Freud, the anarchistic philosophy of Nietzsche). For the purposes of rethinking evangelical theology, however, two of these critiques are of particular value. We will first examine Kierkegaard's attack upon "the bewitchment of being" and then Wittgenstein's struggle to exorcise "the bewitchment of language."[9]

---

[8]G. W. F. Hegel, *The Phenomenology of Mind*, 2d ed. rev., trans. J. Baillie (London: George Allan and Unwin, 1949).

[9]For an enlightening comparison of the thought of these two obviously different and yet paradoxically similar philosophers, see Charles L. Creegan, *Wittgenstein and Kierkegaard: Religion, Individuality, and Philosophical Method* (London: Routledge, 1989). I am indebted to Paul L. Holmer for first pointing out this strange and intriguing resemblance to me through his lectures in philosophical theology at Yale Divinity School.

The Bewitchment of Being—Kierkegaard

Søren Kierkegaard ironically dismantles Hegel's philosophical system.[10] Kierkegaard shows how grand metaphysical philosophical systems have been bewitched by the abstract notion of being, which separates thought from individual existence. After all, one cannot "be in general" without being some*thing* (or someone). Truth is not equivalent to the thought of being. Being, without being something, is a figment of the speculative philosopher's imagination. As Kierkegaard contends in *Training in Christianity*, "Truth in its very being is not the duplication of *being* in terms of *thought*, which yields only the *thought of being*."[11]

Anthony Kenny offers the following linguistic analysis of this philosophical bewitchment of being:

> Thus a philosopher may be struck by the fact that whatever exists can be said to *be*; and taking this verb as a copula, or predicate-marker, he may seek to investigate the nature of the attribute corresponding to this predicate which is applicable to everything in the world. He may be struck by the mystery of this *be-ing* which is not *being red* or *being a man*, but just pure *be-ing*. He may even deify his muddle by defining God as Pure Being.[12]

According to Kierkegaard, metaphysical speculation that links God and Being in the abstract has led Christians into the "monstrous illusion" of confusing thought about God with existence in the truth, thus creating the spectre of a "Christendom" that prevents discipleship. The Johannine vision of "being the truth" has

---

[10]See particularly Kierkegaard's satirically titled *Concluding Unscientific Postscript*, trans. David F. Swenson and Walter Lowrie (Princeton: Princeton University Press, 1941).

[11]Trans. Walter Lowrie (Princeton: Princeton University Press, 1967, c. 1941) 201.

[12]Anthony Kenny, *Wittgenstein* (London: Penguin Books, 1973). Kenny is here illustrating the usefulness of a formal logical script like Frege's *Begriffsschrift* in Wittgenstein's early philosophy (cf. *Tractatus Logico-Philosophicus* 3.323).

been lost in the false Cartesian dichotomy between subject and object.[13] As Kierkegaard proclaims,

> And hence, Christianly understood, the truth consists not in knowing the truth but in being the truth. . . . For knowing the truth is something which follows as a matter of course from being the truth, and not conversely; and precisely for this reason it becomes untruth when knowing the truth is separated from being the truth, or when knowing the truth is treated as one and the same thing as being the truth.[14]

Kierkegaard's critique of speculative metaphysics based upon the thought of being challenges the foundations of all of those theological systems which link together God and Being. Kierkegaard raises the question whether the ontological "foundation" upon which these "palaces of thought" are built is anything more than a sand-castle illusion. Have these theologians been bewitched by the thought of Being? Shouldn't Christian theology instead focus upon the meaning of individual Christian existence as portrayed in the difficult task of truly becoming a Christian disciple?[15] Kierkegaard's critique offers the salutary reminder that theology should be rooted in the life of faith, rather than in a speculative metaphysical system.

The Bewitchment of Language—Wittgenstein

Kierkegaard's explicitly Christian critique of the bewitchment of being in speculative metaphysics is paralleled by Ludwig Wittgenstein's nonconfessional critique of the bewitchment of language in

---

[13]A good illustration of this subject-object dichotomy in relation to the theological issue of authority is provided by P. T. Forsyth's assertion that, "The real ground of our certitude, therefore, is the nature of the thing of which we are sure, rather than the nature of the experience in which we are sure. . . . It is what we are sure of that enables us to say why we are sure of it" (*The Principle of Authority*, 48).

[14]Kierkegaard, *Training in Christianity*, 201.

[15]As critics have repeatedly pointed out, the weakness of Kierkegaard's existentialism lies here in its ignoring or downplaying the wider issues of community and culture in the formation of Christian identity.

Western philosophy.[16] While Kierkegaard's approach to truth is individualistic and private, Wittgenstein's direction is more public and communal.

In a famous remark Wittgenstein asserted, "Philosophy is a battle against the bewitchment [*Verhexung*] of our intelligence [*Verstandes*] by means of language."[17] Anthony Kenny observes that,

> there is a philosopher in each of us, against whom we need to be on our guard: we must, if the occasion arises, exorcise the bad implicit philosophy which we imbibe unknowingly as we acquire language; philosophy will enable us to avoid this bewitchment to which we are subject as to an original sin.[18]

Fergus Kerr argued convincingly in *Theology after Wittgenstein*[19] that much of Wittgenstein's work may be understood as a struggle to exorcise the Cartesian mentalist "ghost in the machine" with its false choice between philosophical idealism and realism.[20] As Kerr summarized Wittgenstein's quest,

> We have been tempted into the habit of thinking that either *die Dinge* or *unsere Vorstellungen* must be the primary thing, but the choice between realism and idealism overlooks *das Leben*: that is Wittgenstein's suggestion.[21]

Our language has been bewitched by the illusion that "real meaning" lies only inside our minds in a private world apart from the public transactions of ordinary conversation. Wittgenstein instead exhorted:

---

[16]For a lucid general introduction to Wittgenstein's difficult thought, see David Pears, *Wittgenstein*, Fontana Modern Masters Series, ed. Frank Kermode (Glasgow: Collins, 1971).

[17]Ludwig Wittgenstein, *Philosophische Untersuchungen/ Philosophical Investigations*, [hereafter referred to as *PI*] trans. G. E. M. Anscombe (Oxford: Basil Blackwell, 1963) I: 109.

[18]Anthony Kenny, *The Legacy of Wittgenstein* (Oxford: Basil Blackwell, 1984) xi.

[19]Fergus Kerr, *Theology after Wittgenstein* (Oxford: Basil Blackwell, 1986).

[20]Thus philosophical empiricism also is challenged by Wittgenstein's approach.

[21]Kerr, *Theology*, 133.

> Try not to think of understanding as a "mental process" at all, for *that* is the expression which confuses you. But ask yourself: in what sort of case, in what kind of circumstances, do we say, "Now I know how to go on, . . ."[22]

We are so preoccupied with the subject-object dichotomy between "what is going on in our heads" and "what is going on in the world" that we fail to look at the actual workings of our forms of speech, where meaning is shaped. Paul Holmer aptly described this predicament:

> A kind of spiritualization of language takes place among us, and most of that finds its fruition in a notion that the realm of meaning is mentalistic, inside of our heads, and finally the sort of place or region to which a person has only his private and highly privileged access. For if we "mean" . . . by some kind of intentional activity like thinking or knowing ("I know what I mean"), then there is no public and ruled access to anything but the sound and shape of the words.[23]

The alliance between classical metaphysical categories and Cartesian theology is thus under assault on two fronts. First, the linkage of the language of Being with language about God is vulnerable to the charge of reification, particularly in a culture that finds metaphysical ontology suspect. Second, the mentalist perspective on meaning assumes a Cartesian subject-object dichotomy, which ignores the actual operation of meanings in ordinary conversation.

These critiques of the bewitchment of being and language cast serious doubt upon the classical philosophical categories which have shaped the language of theology. The continued use of metaphysical categories to formulate the doctrines of the Christian faith would seem to be a dubious course for the future welfare of evangelical theology.[24] Theological reliance upon doubtful philosophical

---

[22]*PI*, I, 154.

[23]Paul L. Holmer, "Language and Theology," in *The Grammar of Faith* (San Francisco: Harper and Row, 1978) 119.

[24]For a parade example of a strenuous contemporary effort to continue the use of Aristotelian categories in conservative Protestant theology, see Carl F.H. Henry, *God, Revelation, and Authority*, 6 vols. (Waco TX: Word, 1976–1983).

"foundations" could result in an anachronistic theology, which parades around in an embarrassing state, like the vain ruler in "The Emperor's New Clothes"!

The remainder of this chapter is devoted to the examination of two sorts of alternatives: (1) the hermeneutically restructured categories of Gadamer and Ricoeur and (2) the postcritical categories of Wittgenstein. Though distinct from each other, these two loose groupings may be understood as overlapping streams of cross-disciplinary hermeneutics.[25] Both groupings represent hermeneutical alternatives to the traditional alliance between classical metaphysics and Cartesian theology. Both are particularly helpful in providing philosophical categories for illuminating and modifying Childs' canonical hermeneutics.

· Hermeneutically Restructured Categories ·

In response to the critique of Enlightenment conceptuality, a number of contemporary theologians have turned to philosophical hermeneutics for more dynamic categories in which to ground the language of theology. David Tracy defends this shift:

> The [systematic] theologian's task must be primarily hermeneutical. Yet this is not equivalent to being unconcerned with truth, unless "truth" is exhaustively defined on strictly Enlightenment and increasingly instrumental terms. Rather the theologian by risking faith in a particular religious tradition, has the right and responsibility to be "formed" by that tradition and community.[26]

---

[25]I am not, of course, claiming here that these two groupings represent any more than a small portion of the vast and relatively disordered field of contemporary hermeneutics. I have chosen them principally for their utility in illuminating and modifying Childs' canonical hermeneutics. I have collaborated with William L. Hendricks in the compiling of an annotated teaching bibliography of theological hermeneutics. For one helpful introductory construal of the field, see Josef Bleicher, *Contemporary Hermeneutics: Hermeneutics as Method, Philosophy and Critique* (Boston: Routledge and Kegan Paul, 1980).

[26]David Tracy, "The Necessity and Insufficiency of Fundamental Theology," in *Problems and Perspectives of Fundamental Theology*, ed. René Latourelle and Gerald O'Collins, trans. Matthew J. O'Connell (New York: Paulist Press, 1982) 23-36 at 34-35.

This hermeneutical shift in theology is particularly characterized by the rejection of a subject-object dichotomy that is linked to a supposedly objective scientific method. The philosophical assumptions underlying the historical-critical method are radically challenged, with the result that the foundations of theologies built upon reconstructed history begin to crumble.[27]

In this situation, a new understanding and reappropriation of the traditions that constitute and sustain religious communities are in order. Hans-Georg Gadamer's hermeneutical notion of tradition offers a helpful complement to Wittgenstein's focus upon the use of language and a useful approach to the challenge of reappropriating the historical traditions of the Christian faith.[28]

Tradition and Language—Gadamer

In his *magnum opus, Truth and Method*, Gadamer reveals the essential connection between tradition and language: *"Das Wesen der Überlieferung durch Sprachlichkeit charakterisiert ist."*[29] Gadamer emphasizes the role of "language as the medium of hermeneutical experience (*Erfahrung*)."[30] Traditions become meaningful through an ongoing process of interpretation, which follows the model of "conversation" or "dialogue" (*Gespräch*).[31] A text like the Bible is not an historical relic—a collection of "facts" to be dissected

---

[27]See the discussion of "The Material Problem: The Decline of the Historical-Critical Paradigm" in the first chapter for further illustration of this state of affairs.

[28]For discussion of how Gadamer's understanding of tradition might complement Wittgenstein's concept of language games, see the section "Forms of Life and Language Games" at the end of this chapter.

[29]Hans-Georg Gadamer, *Wahrheit und Methode*, [hereafter WM] 2nd ed. (Tübingen: J. C. B. Mohr, 1965) 367; E. T. *Truth and Method*, [hereafter TM] ed. Garrett Barden and John Cumming (New York: Seabury Press, 1975). The English translation "tradition is linguistic in character" (*TM*, 351) lacks the emphasis of the German original.

[30]WM, 361-82; TM, 345-66.

[31]WM, 351-60, 363-67; TM, 333-41, 347-51.

through analysis.[32] Rather, the text is a living tradition that "speaks" to the experience of the interpreter in both positive and negative fashion. As Gadamer contends,

> At the beginning of all historical hermeneutics, then, *the abstract antithesis between tradition and historical research [Historie], between history [Geschichte] and knowledge [Wissen] must be discarded.*[33] The effect [*Wirkung*] of a living tradition and the effect of historical study must constitute a unity [*Wirkungseinheit*], the analysis of which would reveal only a texture [*Geflecht*] of reciprocal relationships [*Wechselwirkungen*]. Hence we would do well not to regard historical consciousness as something radically new—as it seems at first—but as a new element [*Moment*] within that which has always made up the human relation to the past. In other words, we have to recognize the element of tradition in the historical relation and enquire into its hermeneutical productivity.[34]

Although Gadamer's hermeneutical notion of tradition is set in the framework of idealistic ontology, thus rendering Gadamer liable to the charge of succumbing to the bewitchment of being and language described above, the usefulness of his hermeneutical notion of tradition is not automatically invalidated.[35] The appropriation of Gadamer's emphasis upon the connection of tradition and language does not necessarily entail the adoption of his philosophical idealism.

For instance, in the first part of *Truth and Method*, Gadamer uses the model of playing a game (*Spiel*) as a guide (*Leitfaden*) to understanding aesthetic consciousness.[36] The unintentional resemblance to Wittgenstein's notion of language games (discussed later in this chapter) is so striking that it occasions this remarkable

---

[32]Gadamer's view is in direct contradiction to the rationalist epistemology that underlies much (but not all) conservative evangelical and fundamentalist theology. As B. B. Warfield asserts, "What Christianity consists in is facts that are doctrines, and doctrines that are facts" (*The Right of Systematic Theology* [Edinburgh: T. & T. Clark, 1897]) 34.

[33]Emphasis on this clause is included in the German original, which emphasizes the "disintegration" [*Auflösung*] of the antithesis.

[34]*WM*, 267; *TM*, 251.

[35]See particularly the section "Language as a horizon of hermeneutic ontology" (*WM*, 415-65; *TM*, 397-447).

[36]*WM*, 97-127; *TM*, 91-119.

footnote in Gadamer's "Foreward to the Second Edition": "Wittgenstein's concept of 'language games' seemed quite natural to me when I came across it."[37]

Gadamer elsewhere claims,

> Something like a convergence is occurring between Wittgenstein's critique of Anglo-Saxon semantics on the one hand, and the criticism of the ahistorical art of phenomenological description that is made by . . . hermeneutical consciousness [in Gadamer's work] on the other.[38]

Thus, Gadamer's hermeneutical notion of tradition, with its fundamental connection to language, may be adapted to epistemological traditions (like those of Wittgenstein) that reject his idealist ontology.

Another aspect of Gadamer's understanding of tradition that has proven useful to theologians is his idea of "the classic."[39] In Gadamer's view, "the word 'classical' means . . . [that] the duration of the power of a work to speak directly [*unmittelbaren*] is

---

[37]*TM*, 500, n. 12.

[38]Hans-Georg Gadamer, *Philosophical Hermeneutics*, trans. David E. Linge (Berkeley: University of California Press, 1976) 127. I am indebted to Anthony Thiselton for drawing my attention to this remark by Gadamer. For further comparisons see Thiselton's *The Two Horizons: New Testament Hermeneutics and Philosophical Description with Special Reference to Heidegger, Bultmann, Gadamer and Wittgenstein* (Exeter: Paternoster Press, 1980), esp. 33-40.

[39]David Tracy has adapted and extended Gadamer's concept of "the classic" into a major hermeneutical foundation for systematic theology (David Tracy, *The Analogical Imagination: Christian Theology and the Culture of Pluralism* [New York: Crossroad, 1981], especially ch 3, "The Classic," 99-153). For Tracy's discussion in this work of his differences from Gadamer, see especially 35-36, n. 8. Tracy offers a brief, lucid introduction to Gadamer's hermeneutics in "Interpretation of the Bible and Interpretation Theory," in Robert M. Grant with David Tracy, *A Short History of the Interpretation of the Bible*, 2d ed. (Philadelphia: Fortress Press, 1984) 154-60.

fundamentally unlimited."[40] Like Luther's notion of Scripture,[41] the classical interprets itself.[42]

Avery Dulles offers an overview of the implications of the theo- logical application of Gadamer's view to the Bible.

> The distinctive character of a classical or canonical text, as Hans-Georg Gadamer has shown, is its ability to interpret itself and to say something to every generation. The Bible, as a canonical text, is not just a quarry of materials to be shaped according to the perspective of the reader. . . . The Bible forms the consciousness of its own readers, brings its own horizon with it, and thereby shapes a tradition of interpretation. The Christian reader, dwelling within that tradition, will allow the Bible to establish its own framework of meaning, forming, reforming, and trans- forming its readers.[43]

Thus, when separated from its idealist ontology, Gadamer's her- meneutical notion of tradition offers an historically-shaped and dialogically-formed dynamic to an evangelical theology seeking lib- eration from its own Cartesian captivity to a dead historicism.[44]

Now we turn to another philosophical approach utilizing her- meneutically restructured categories, as we examine Paul Ricoeur's emphasis upon the recovery of levels of meaning.[45]

---

[40]*WM*, 274; *TM*, 258.

[41]"*Scriptura . . . sui ipsius interpres*" (Martin Luther, *Assertio omnium articulorum M. Lutheri per bullam Leonis X novissimam damnatorum*, in *D. Martin Luthers Werke. Kritische Gesamtausgabe* [Weimar: Böhlau, 1897], vol. 7, 97).

[42]*WM*, 273-74; *TM*, 257. Gadamer here cites Hegel rather than Luther as the source of his view.

[43]Dulles, *Models of Revelation*, 209-10.

[44]I am using the phrase "dead historicism" here to refer to a postivistic understanding of "scientific history," which claims a fixed objectivity. Such a view is challenged by Gadamer's dynamic understanding of "effective history."

[45]Ricoeur's approach offers some valuable correctives to criticisms of Gadamer's tradition-bound idealism or "historicism" that have been offered by the Frankfurt School and other exponents of "critical hermeneutics." For an intro- duction to the early stages of this debate, see Bleicher, *Contemporary Hermeneutics*.

Reading and Levels of Meaning—Ricoeur

Ricoeur has advocated a dialectical theory of reading that overcomes the opposition between structuralism and critical theory.[46] Language is "composed of a hierarchy of levels."[47] Reading is then seen as a process that works on this series of levels for the "recovery of meaning," uniting the poles of "understanding" and "explanation" into a "hermeneutical arc." In his essay, "What is a Text? Explanation and Understanding" Ricoeur summarizes this process as follows:[48]

> If . . . we regard structural analysis as a stage—and a necessary one—between a naive and critical interpretation, between a surface and depth interpretation, then it seems possible to situate explanation and interpretation along a unique hermeneutical arc and to integrate the opposed attitudes of explanation and understanding within an overall concept of reading as the recovery of meaning.[49]

Ricoeur sees reading as a dialectical process that begins at "the level of the word" (the semiotic level), where the insights of structuralism are incorporated and then transcended. Next, the reader moves to "the level of the sentence" (the semantic level), where the issues of understanding the meaning of a text come to the fore. Non-literal figures of speech, especially metaphor, play a major

---

[46]Ricoeur offers a helpful introduction to his own approach to hermeneutics in his lectures published as *Interpretation Theory: Discourse and the Surplus of Meaning* (Fort Worth TX: Texas Christian University Press, 1976). The reader interested in pursuing Ricoeur's analysis of structuralism and its limits should examine the essays collected under the title *The Conflict of Interpretations: Essays in Hermeneutics*, ed. Don Ihde (Evanston, IL: Northwestern Univ. Press, 1974), especially 44-61 and 79-96.

[47]Paul Ricoeur, "Structure, Word, Event," trans. Robert Sweeney, in *The Conflict of Interpretations*, 80.

[48]In *Hermeneutics and the Human Sciences*, trans. John B. Thompson (Cambridge: Cambridge University Press, 1981), 145-64. For the French original see Paul Ricoeur, "Qu'est-ce qu'une texte? expliquer et comprendre," in *Hermeneutik und Dialektik: Aufsätze*, ed. R. Bubner, K. Cramer, and R. Wiehl, 2 vols. (Tübingen: J.C. B. Mohr, 1970) 2: 181-200.

[49]Ibid., 161.

role here.[50] Finally, the reader moves to "the level of discourse" (sometimes called the hermeneutical level), where issues of genre (e.g., history and fiction) affect the meaning of texts.[51] At this level Ricoeur tackles the perennial issues (*aporias*) of temporality, including the development of his mimetic approach to historical intentionality.

Ricoeur's hermeneutical restructuring of the category of "levels of meaning" opens a way for dialogue with the traditions of pre-critical interpretation. The history of exegesis, with its famous "fourfold sense" of Scripture,[52] has a long acquaintance with hermeneutical control of levels of meaning, which should not be ignored.[53]

At the beginning of the first volume of *Time and Narrative* Ricoeur creatively uses Augustine's analysis of the experience of time in Book XI of the *Confessions* as a foundation for a post-Heideggerian analysis of the phenomenology of time.[54]

According to Ricoeur, the "originality" of Heidegger's understanding of time lies in its "hierarchization of levels of temporality"—a move that Augustine foreshadowed when he "gave credit in advance to the idea of temporal levels."[55]

---

[50]See Ricoeur's detailed work, *The Rule of Metaphor: Multi-Disciplinary Studies of the Creation of Meaning in Language,* trans. Robert Czerny (Toronto: University of Toronto Press, 1977) for the development of this approach to semantics. See especially p. 3 for Ricoeur's own description of these levels of meaning in his hermeneutical philosophy.

[51]Ricoeur's three-volume synthesis, *Time and Narrative,* trans. Kathleen McLaughlin/Blamey and David Pellauer (Chicago: University of Chicago Press, 1984, 1985, 1988) addresses this third level.

[52]For detailed documentation of this tradition see Henri de Lubac's monumental *Exégèse médiévale: Le quatre sens de l'Écriture,* 2 vols. in 4 (Paris: Aubier, 1959-1964).

[53]See David Steinmetz, "The Superiority of Pre-Critical Exegesis," *Theology Today* 37 (1980): 27-38, for a provocative and controversial statement of this concern.

[54]Ricoeur, *Time and Narrative,* 1:5-30.

[55]Ibid., 84. The larger context of these quotations offers a more complete summary of the technical details of Ricoeur's argument: "The properly phenomenological originality of the Heideggerian analysis of time—an originality due entirely to its anchorage in an ontology of Care—consists of a hierarchization of the levels of temporality or rather of temporalization. Having shown this, we shall

In his study of Freud, Ricoeur also makes the temporally-based distinction between "the archaeology" and "the teleology" of the text.[56] These time-based levels of meaning can prove helpful for the task of distinguishing between the historical process of the formation of the Bible into a canonical text and its subsequent and continuing theological interpretation by communities of faith.[57]

The history of "precritical" Christian biblical interpretation is characterized by methods such as typology and allegory, which use levels of time and eternity to ground various levels of meaning. This pattern may be discovered in the classical fourfold levels, which move from the "historical or literal level" (the past) to the "allegorical level" (connecting past and present) to the "moral or tropological level" (what shall be done in the present and immediate future) to the "mystical or anagogical level" (the future of eternity).[58]

The significance of Ricoeur's emphasis upon levels of meaning for canonical hermeneutics becomes apparent in the next chapter when we examine the different levels of meaning in a theological commentary like Brevard Childs' *The Book of Exodus*.[59] Another aspect of Ricoeur's hermeneutical theory, his mimetic view of historical intentionality, is also of such significance in modifying Childs' approach that it is worth introducing in this context.

In the first volume of *Time and Narrative*, Ricoeur argues for the rehabilitation of "that fundamental noetic vision of history . . .

---

be able to discover a presentiment of this theme in Augustine. Indeed by interpreting the existence of time in terms of distention and by describing human time as raised beyond its inside by the attraction of its polar opposite, eternity, Augustine gave credit in advance to the idea of temporal levels."

[56]Paul Ricoeur, *Freud and Philosophy: An Essay in Interpretation*, trans. Denis Savage (New Haven: Yale University Press, 1970), especially 419-551.

[57]For further discussion see the section "Scripture and Doctrine: Canon as the Rule of Scripture" in Chapter 4.

[58]I am, of course, not claiming that all exegesis done under the classic fourfold pattern fits into these temporal levels. Rather, I am observing that the general direction of much exegesis done under this method moves from the biblical past to the eternal future. For detailed explanation and examination of these levels see de Lubac, *Exégèse médiévale*.

[59]*The Book of Exodus: A Critical, Theological Commentary*, The Old Testament Library (Philadelphia: Westminster Press, 1974; also London: SCM Press, 1974).

called *historical intentionality.*"[60] Ricoeur holds that there is an *"indirect* connection that must be maintained . . . between history and our narrative competence."[61] He is careful to note that his "thesis concerning the ultimately narrative character of history is in no way to be confused with a defense of narrative history."[62] Ricoeur uses a metaphorical notion of historical intentionality to ground a "vision" of history.[63] Historical intentionality does not refer to the specific intentions of a given author or editor of the texts, nor to the subjective intentions of a given historical agent behind the text, whether personal or structural. For Ricoeur, historical intentionality instead refers to the narrative shape ("configuration") of the texts themselves. The intentionality is embodied in the literary patterns of the texts.

In the act of reading meaning is created by the interaction between the configurations of the text and the perceptions of the readers. Particularly in the reading of ancient texts direct access to the worlds of the authors "behind" the text is impossible, and much historical reconstruction (establishing "the archaeology" of the text) is hypothetical. Therefore, the creation of meaning primarily happens "in front of" the text—namely, in the dialectical interaction between text and its readers.

Having described these selected, hermeneutically restructured categories of Gadamer and Ricoeur, we now examine some post-critical categories arising out of the work of Wittgenstein.

· The Formulation of Postcritical Categories ·

Wittgenstein's later philosophical work, particularly the posthumously published *Philosophical Investigations,* has a constructive as

---

[60]Ricoeur, *Time and Narrative,* I: 229. For Ricoeur's summary of this volume see 226-30.

[61]Ibid., 175.

[62]Ibid., 91.

[63]Cf. also Paul Ricoeur, "Metaphor and the Central Problem of Hermeneutics," in *Hermeneutics and the Human Sciences,* 165-81.

well as a deconstructive side.[64] Besides the further development of
his critique of the bewitchment of language, Wittgenstein proposes
some helpful categories that assist us in clarifying the role and status of canonical hermeneutics in a postcritical evangelical theology.

Meaning as Use and Theology as Grammar

Instead of locating meaning in the private recesses of the "mind"
of the reader or in some reconstructed historical "events" behind
a text, Wittgenstein offers a publically observable, functional definition of meaning.[65]

> For a *large* class of cases—though not for all—in which we employ the
> word "meaning" it can be defined thus: the meaning of a word is its use
> [*Gebrauch*] in language [*Sprache*].[66]

If one wants to know what a word means, one looks at the ways
and contexts in which it is used.

While such a procedure might seem obvious, its practice turns
out to be much more difficult, for we tend to assume that words
have a meaning or meanings, rather than that their usage really
constitutes their meaning. For a dramatic example of this problem
in the biblical field, one need only turn to James Barr's critique of

---

[64]I am not claiming here that Wittgenstein's later work is discontinuous with
his earlier work, but rather am describing some of the new categories that emerge
out of his later writings. For expositions stressing the continuity of Wittgenstein's
philosophical development, see the introductions by David Pears and Anthony
Kenny, previously cited.

[65]Cf. Wittgenstein's comments on the inadequacy of historical facts as a logical
foundation for Christianity: "It has been said that Christianity rests on an historic
basis. It has been said a thousand times by intelligent people that indubitability
is not enough in this case. Even if there is as much evidence as for Napoleon. *Because the indubitability would not be enough to make me change my whole life*. It doesn't
rest on an historic basis in the sense that the ordinary belief in historic facts could
serve as a foundation" (Ludwig Wittgenstein, *Lectures and Conversations on Aesthetics, Psychology and Religious Belief*, ed. Cyril Barrett [Oxford: Basil Blackwell, 1966],
57, emphasis added).

[66]*PI*, I: 43.

the massive Kittel's *Theological Dictionary of the New Testament* for ignoring this distinction.[67]

The "Cartesian ghost" that tells us that the meaning of words is in our heads, not in their application in our speech, is a difficult one to exorcise, as Wittgenstein explains:

> What is essential is to see that the same thing can come before our minds when we hear the word and the application [*Anwendung*] still be different. Has it the *same* meaning both times? I think we shall say not.[68]

If we can shift our focus from the pictures or images that form in our heads when we use words to the concrete ways we use language in our ordinary speech, then we can avoid being bewitched by our language. Such a shift would have major implications for the nature and practice of theology.[69] If theology at its heart concerns the use of our human language (*logos*) about God (*theos*), then the practice of theology should look more like grammar than like speculative reflection. In the words of Wittgenstein's incisive remark: "Grammar tells what kind of object anything is. (Theology as grammar.)"[70]

When a person learns a language, he or she learns the rules for using that language, its grammar. This learning may be implicit (e.g., a child's learning a first language) or explicit (e.g., sitting down with a grammar book), but one cannot learn a language without acquiring at least some of its grammar. As Fergus Kerr comments,

> In effect, by remarking that theology is grammar he [Wittgenstein] is reminding us that it is only by listening to what we say about God (what has been said for many generations), and to how what is said about God ties in with what we say and do in innumerable other

---

[67]James Barr, *The Semantics of Biblical Language* (Oxford: Oxford Univ. Press, 1961), chap. 8, "Some Principles of Kittel's Theological Dictionary," 206-62.

[68]*PI*, I: 140.

[69]See particularly, Paul Holmer's essays, "What Theology Is and Does" and "What Theology Is and Does—Again" (*The Grammar of Faith*, 1-36) for a provocative, practical description of some of these implications.

[70]*PI*, I: 373.

connections, that we have any chance of understanding what we mean when we speak of God.[71]

Moreover, learning grammar is not an end in itself. Rather the object of learning grammar is that one may speak and write grammatically and so be clearly understood by others. After we have long forgotten any explicit grammatical rules that we may have memorized, we still are observing these rules *in practice* whenever we speak and write grammatically.[72]

There are some limitations to Wittgenstein's metaphor of theology as grammar. For instance, grammar doesn't have as controlling a relationship to the content of what we speak as theology does to the language of faith.[73] Nevertheless, Christian doctrine may be conceived in some ways as analogous to good grammar. Doctrine provides the rules—often in the form of negative guidelines—that regulate our talk about God.[74] Learning doctrine is not an end in itself. Rather, just as one learns grammar to speak correctly (i.e., grammatically), so one learns doctrine to speak correctly about God. Just as one learns grammar to communicate clearly with others, so one learns doctrine to communicate clearly about the faith. Wittgenstein's notion of theology as grammar thus provides a fruitful metaphor for conceiving the nature and function of theology.

We now turn to specific expressions of this approach in Wittgenstein's descriptions of language games rooted in forms of life.

---

[71]Kerr, *Theology*, 147-48.

[72]I am particularly indebted to Holmer's essay, "What Theology Is and Does—Again" (*The Grammar of Faith*) for shaping this development of Wittgenstein's analogy.

[73]Another important limitation to Wittgenstein's analogy, which moves beyond the scope of this project, is the relationship of theology as grammar to other forms of Christian language, such as prayer and preaching. Shouldn't these other ruled forms of Christian language be regarded as "the grammar of faith" as well?

[74]George Lindbeck's *The Nature of Doctrine: Religion and Theology in a Postliberal Age* (Philadelphia: Westminster, 1984) develops this regulative notion of doctrine in a "cultural-linguistic" model. The fifth chapter will utilize some aspects of Lindbeck's model to explore a canonical approach to the doctrine of God.

Forms of Life and Language Games

Wittgenstein's enigmatic notion of "forms of life" has been the occasion of much debate, especially in its application to the question of justification of religious belief.[75] Wittgenstein declares: "What has to be accepted, the given, is—so one could say—*forms of life*."[76]

Discussion thus ranges around the matter of how broad a concept one should take "form of life" to be. For instance, could a religious grouping like Baptists or Catholics or Buddhists be a form of life and thus perhaps be exempt from the task of external justification of its beliefs? Generally, recent interpretation has tended to reject this approach in favor of a view that understands "forms of life" to refer to performative activities (small-scale practices) of daily life.[77] Such practices mentioned by Wittgenstein include "hoping"[78] and "being certain."[79] Thus, a religion contains a host of practices that are forms of life.

For theological reflection the most important aspect of religious forms of life is their connection with religious language. Wittgenstein describes this relationship using his category of language games.[80] "The term *language-game* is meant to bring into prominence the fact that the *speaking* of language is part of an activity, or of a form of life."[81] In Wittgenstein's use, language games are not frivolous entertainment, but the patterned uses that we make

---

[75]For a summary of this debate into the early 1970s, see Alan Keightley, *Wittgenstein, Grammar and God* (London: Epworth Press, 1976), 31-37. For more recent discussion, see Kerr, *Theology*, especially 29-31, and Placher, *Unapologetic Theology*, especially 57-62.

[76]*PI*, II: 226. The term "form of life" appears only four other times in *Philosophical Investigations* (I: 19, 23, and 241; II, 174).

[77]See particularly Patrick Sherry, "Is Religion a 'Form of Life'?" *American Philosophical Quarterly*, 9 (1972): 159-67, cited in Keightley, 33; and Kerr, *Theology*, 29-31 and 64-65. Also, for the extension of this debate to language games see Nicholas Lash, "How Large is a 'Language Game'?" *Theology*, 87 (1984): 19-28.

[78]*PI*, II: 174.

[79]Ludwig Wittgenstein, *On Certainty* (Oxford: Basil Blackwell, 1969) 358.

[80]At the beginning of *Philosophical Investigations*, (I: 7) Wittgenstein offers the following definition: "I shall call the whole, consisting of language and the actions into which it is woven, the 'language game.' "

[81]*PI*, I: 23.

of language. Perhaps a "game of chess" might illustrate the complexity embraced by the concept, while a modern army's "war game" or the "game of Russian roulette" might show its applicability to life-and-death matters. The central insight is the change of perspective from the dichotomy of internal consciousness and external observation to the wholeness of patterned (rule-governed) interactions.

Fergus Kerr vividly portrays this shift of perspective:

> At the outset [of *Philosophical Investigations*] we are reminded that we are agents in practical intercourse with one another—not solitary observers gazing upwards to the celestial realm of the eternal forms, or inwards at the show in the mental theater. What constitutes us as human beings is the regular and patterned reactions we have to one another. It is in our dealings with each other—in how we *act*—that human life is founded.[82]

As David Tracy has noted, one of the limitations of Wittgenstein's concept of language games is his failure to pay enough attention to the *relationships between* language games.[83] Wittgenstein's understanding of the patterned interactions of language games creates a space where Gadamer's hermeneutical notion of tradition[84] can help to explain the historical process of the traditioning of language games.[85] Gadamer's emphasis upon community created by dialogue can enrich Wittgenstein's view of rule-governed language games. So Wittgenstein's linguistic framework might be expanded to accommodate the historical traditions of the scriptural interpretation of religious communities.

Having grasped this hermeneutically enriched view of language games, it is very easy for readers of Wittgenstein to fall into the trap of confusing the *context-dependence* and community-shaping of language games with the naive assertion of philosophical

---

[82]Kerr, *Theology*, 65.

[83]David Tracy, *Plurality and Ambiguity* (San Francisco: Harper and Row, 1987) 115, n.6.

[84]See the section "Tradition and Language-Gadamer" for an exposition of this idea in Gadamer.

[85]I am grateful to Dan Stiver for first pointing out to me this possible interrelationship between Gadamer's and Wittgenstein's diverse philosophical approaches.

relativism. If there is no independent standpoint from which all truth can be known, then is not everything simply reduced to individual "interpretation"—with one interpretation as good as the next? Wittgenstein, however, plainly declares that "Interpretations by themselves [*allein*] do not determine meaning."[86] He proceeds to describe the "paradox" that falsely entices people to relativism:

> This was our paradox: no course of action could be determined by a rule, because every course of action could be made out to accord with the rule. The answer was: if everything can be made out to accord with the rule, then it can also be made out to conflict with it. And so there would be neither accord nor conflict here.[87]

Religious persons who accept a "rule" (canon) of Scripture may find this "paradox" to be quite familiar. For example, how many times have Christians been informed by their critics that, since the Bible must be interpreted, "every course of action could be made out to accord with the rule"? Is it correct that any interpretation of the Scripture can truly be justified? Wittgenstein thinks that such relativism is a misunderstanding of the operation of language games:

> It can be seen that there is a misunderstanding here from the mere fact that in the course of our argument we give one interpretation after another; as if each one contented us at least for the moment, until we thought of yet another standing behind it. What this shows is that there is a way of grasping a rule which is *not* an *interpretation* [*Deutung*], but which is exhibited in what we call "obeying the rule" and "going against it" in actual cases.
> Hence there is an inclination to say: every action according to the rule is an interpretation. But we ought to restrict the term "interpretation" to the substitution of one expression of the rule for another.[88]

Therefore, the context-dependence and community-shaping of language games is to be carefully distinguished from an atomistic relativism, which assumes that any one language game contains its

---

[86]*PI*, I: 198.
[87]*PI*, I: 201.
[88]Ibid.

own internal meaning and is as true or false as any other. Accusations of "Wittgensteinian fideism" frequently attribute such a misinterpretation of Wittgenstein to theologians who make use of his categories.[89]

W. Donald Hudson offers a lucid summary of the relationship between truth and language games in Wittgenstein:

> What counts as the truth or falsity of a proposition, and what counts as a valid reason for saying something, depends on the language-game within which the proposition is stated or the reason is offered. The belief that there is a truth which can be known or a rationality which can be apprehended *outside all language-games* and by which their respective truth and rationality can be decided is misconceived. But it does not follow that therefore any individual language-game (or set of games) can be isolated from the rest and regarded as a logically self-contained unit, so that no considerations except internal ones are relevant to its meaningfulness, truth or rationality.[90]

Thus, for Wittgenstein what is true is contextually dependent upon (and thus *shaped* within) language games rooted in forms of life. This dependence, however, is *not* the contextual determination of relativism, but rather the patterned interactions of rule-shaped practices.

The role of community in forming, shaping, and sustaining these rule-shaped practices is clearly evident throughout the long history of the interpretation of the Scriptures. Central to evangelical theology is the primacy of the Scriptures as the rule-making rule (the *norma normans*)[91] of the community.

Wittgenstein's terminology of language games and forms of life provides us with some valuable categories for illuminating the role

---

[89]As Placher observes, "Wittgensteinian fideism is one of those odd positions which sometimes seem not to have any adherents. When [Kai] Nielsen and others define the position, most of those they might seem to be describing quickly respond, 'But I don't believe *that* at all' " (*Unapologetic Theology*, 61).

[90]W. Donald Hudson, *Wittgenstein and Religious Belief* (London: Macmillan, 1975) 67.

[91]For discussion of this background belief about the role of Scripture in at least some Christian communities, see the section entitled "Disorder in the Garden: The Theologian's Dilemma" in Chapter 1.

of the canon of Scripture in Christian theology. The complex historical language games involved in the interpretation of Scripture by Christian communities are central to their Christian identity. *In evangelical theology the canon of Scripture may be understood as the norm for language games rooted in the practices of Christian forms of life.*

Making such a claim for canon locates evangelical theology on a middle ground. Canonical hermeneutics is neither an expression of the epistemological imperialism of biblical fundamentalism,[92] nor is it merely another example of the relativism of contemporary Western culture. Instead an understanding of the canon of Scripture as the norm for language games rooted in the life of faith communities points toward a way in which the universal truth claims of Scripture are embodied within the concrete, rule-shaped practices of the forms of life of evangelical Christian communities.

In this chapter we have examined some inadequacies of the classical metaphysical categories traditionally linked with Christian theology. We especially noted the critiques of Kierkegaard and Wittgenstein exposing the dangers of the bewitchment of being and language. We then explored the hermeneutically restructured categories of Gadamer and Ricoeur with particular attention to their utility for illuminating canonical hermeneutics. Our discussion focused upon Gadamer's hermeneutical notion of tradition (freed from its background of idealist ontology) and Ricoeur's recovery of levels of meaning and his mimetic understanding of historical intentionality. Finally, we examined some ways in which Wittgenstein's postcritical categories, complemented by Gadamer's emphasis upon communities of interpretation, might offer a philosophical approach to canonical hermeneutics. If we take a functional approach to meaning, theology may be understood as playing a role something like that of the "grammar" of faith. Within evangelical theology canon may be understood as the norm for language games related to Christian forms of life.

---

[92]See James Barr's impassioned attacks on the inadequacy of fundamentalist biblical interpretation and theology, *Fundamentalism* (London: SCM Press, 1977) and *Escaping from Fundamentalism* (London: SCM Press, 1984). For a more moderate critique see John Barton, *People of the Book? The Authority of the Bible in Christianity* (London: SPCK, 1988).

Having completed these philosophical prologues, in the next chapter we turn to the central task of this book—an exposition of Childs' canonical approach to biblical interpretation and the proposal of a number of modifications in response to criticisms it has received.

CANON: CHILDS' APPROACH
TO BIBLICAL INTERPRETATION

The goal of this chapter is the development of a carefully modified version of the canonical hermeneutics of Brevard Childs. First, Childs' canonical approach to biblical interpretation is described in considerable detail. Particular attention is given to three issues: (1) Childs' definition of canon, (2) the emphasis upon the final form of the biblical text, and (3) the concept of the canonical shape of Scripture. Then, in order to help the reader gain a clearer understanding of the approach, three exegetical examples of Childs' interpretation are briefly surveyed. Central themes from Childs' exegesis of the books of Deuteronomy, Exodus, and Ephesians in the context of the canon are displayed.

Childs' formal proposal of his approach through the publication of introductions to the Old and New Testaments was greeted with widespread international discussion and criticism.[1] Unfortunately, a number of the responses reflected misunderstanding of Childs' approach, even to the point of caricature.[2] The latter portion of this chapter is devoted to examining four major criticisms of Childs' work that seem to be valuable: (1) the exclusion of the deuterocanonical books from the Old Testament canon, (2) the inadequacy of Childs' account of tradition, (3) the problematic notion of canonical intentionality, and (4) the need to include new sociological and literary approaches to biblical

---

[1]I have undertaken a detailed survey of the international scholarly response to Childs' proposal in "Canonical Hermeneutics: The Theological Basis and Implications of the Thought of Brevard S. Childs" (Ph.D. dissertation, Southern Baptist Theological Seminary, 1987), especially chapters 1-3.

[2]For example, James Barr's *Holy Scripture: Canon, Authority, Criticism* (Oxford: Oxford University Press, 1983) provides a strongly rhetorical and highly critical evaluation of Childs' Old Testament interpretation, which E. P. Sanders and John Drury echo in their reviews of Childs' New Testament introduction (E. P. Sanders, "Taking It All for Gospel," *Times Literary Supplement*, Dec. 13, 1985, 1431; and John Drury, *Theology*, 89 [1986], 60-62).

interpretation. I seek to demonstrate how canonical hermeneutics may be modified to take account of these significant criticisms.

· Description ·

Childs offers a re-visioning of the task of biblical interpretation, rather than simply another historical-critical methodology. He thus prefers using the terminology "canonical approach" to interpretation or "exegesis in a canonical context," which accommodates this broader point of view. Childs specifically avoids the terms "canon criticism" or "canonical criticism"[3] to describe his perspective, as these terms suggest the formulation of a new method to add to others already associated with the historical-critical approach. Given this broader agenda, how does Childs use the term "canon"?

The Definition of Canon

In his 1977 essay, "The Exegetical Significance of Canon for the Study of the Old Testament," Childs offers the following definition of "canon."

> I am using the term "canon" to refer to that historical process within ancient Israel—particularly in the post-exilic period—which entailed a collecting, selecting, and ordering of texts to serve a normative function as Sacred Scripture within the continuing religious community.[4]

The development of canon is a historical process with an explicitly theological function. As Childs declares,

---

[3]This term is also closely associated with the work of James Sanders, whose use of existentialist hermeneutics is theologically quite divergent from Childs' perspective. See Sanders' *Canon and Community: A Guide to Canonical Criticism* (Philadelphia: Fortress Press, 1984) and *From Sacred Story to Sacred Text* (Philadelphia: Fortress Press, 1987).

[4]Ninth IOSOT *Congress Volume*, Göttingen, 1977, ed. J.A. Emerton *et al.*, *Supplement to Vetus Testamentum*, 29 (Leiden: Brill, 1978) 66-80, at 67.

To speak of the Bible as canon is to emphasize its function as the Word of God in the context of the worshipping community of faith. The canon seeks to preserve the authority of the whole witness and to resist all attempts to assign varying degrees of theological value to the different layers of Scripture on the basis of literary or historical judgments.[5]

Thus, in the example of the last oracles of the book of Amos, which we examined in the first chapter, the historical judgment that these salvation oracles were not part of the historical Amos' original prophecy should *not* mean that they are seen to be "secondary" or of peripheral value to the message of the book.[6] Instead, according to Childs,

The effect of the canonical shaping of ch. 9 is to place Amos' words of judgment within a larger theological framework, which, on the one hand, confirms the truth of Amos' prophecy of doom, and, on the other hand, encompasses it within the promise of God's will for hope and final redemption.[7]

Childs' understanding of canon is not restricted to Christian theological appropriation of the Hebrew Bible. Rather, such an approach can explicitly include Jewish interpretation. From a traditional Jewish perspective, Sid Z. Leiman offers a definition of canon that is congruent with Childs' view. According to Leiman,

A canonical book is accepted by Jews as authoritative for religious practice and/or doctrine, and whose authority is binding upon the Jewish people for all generations. Furthermore, such books are to be studied and expounded in private and in public.[8]

---

[5]"The Canonical Shape of the Prophetic Literature," *Interpretation*, 32 (1978): 46-55, at 53.

[6]See the discussion of Amos 9:11-15 in the section entitled, "The Material Problem: The Decline of the Historical-Critical Paradigm."

[7]Childs, *IOTS*, 407-408.

[8]Sid Z. Leiman, *The Canonization of Hebrew Scripture: The Talmudic and Midrashic Evidence* (Hamden CT: Archon Books, 1976), 14. Leiman follows the rabbinic distinction between inspiration and canonicity in this definition. An inspired book is "composed under divine inspiration"; a canonical book (i.e., one considered "authoritative for religious doctrine and practice") may or may not be inspired (Sid Z. Leiman, "Inspiration and Canonicity: Reflections on the Formation of the Biblical Canon," in *Jewish and Christian Self-Definition*, vol. 2, ed.

What is perhaps the strongest challenge to Childs' definition of canon arises from the historical work of Albert C. Sundberg, Jr.[9] In the process of laying to rest the old Alexandrian canon hypothesis, Sundberg posits a sharp distinction between "Scripture" and "canon."[10] According to Sundberg, the term "canon" refers only to a "closed collection of Scripture."[11] Sundberg thus uses "canon" to refer only to the final stages of what Childs views as the long historical process of the formation of canon. Childs uses the term "canonization" to describe these final phases of fixing the boundaries of canon.

Sundberg's sharp distinction between Scripture and canon serves at least two purposes: (1) the separation of the concept of canon from the historical process of the origin and development of Scripture and (2) the buttressing of his arguments for the inclusion of the books of the Apocrypha (i.e., what Roman Catholics and others have more precisely labeled as "the deuterocanonical books") in the Protestant canon.[12]

Later in this chapter I argue that Childs' canonical approach can be modified to include a place for the deuterocanonical books, based upon the evidence of their use by the early Christian church. Such inclusion, however, should *not* be made dependent upon the positing of a sharp divide between Scripture and canon, which results in the isolation of the development of the Christian canon from the development of the Jewish canon. Sundberg reveals the

---

E. P. Sanders [Philadelphia: Fortress Press, 1981] 56-63, 316-18, at 63.)

[9]Sundberg's major research on this topic may be found in his revised dissertation, *The Old Testament of the Early Church*, Harvard Theological Studies 20 (Cambridge MA: Harvard University Press, 1964). See also an earlier article summarizing his work, "The Old Testament in the Early Church (A Study of Canon)" *Harvard Theological Review* 51 (1958): 205-26.

[10]For a recent restatement of Sundberg's distinction, see Lee Martin McDonald, *The Formation of the Christian Biblical Canon* (Nashville: Abingdon, 1988) 35-47, especially 43-44.

[11]Albert C. Sundberg, Jr., "The 'Old Testament': A Christian Canon," *Catholic Biblical Quarterly* 30 (1968): 143-55, at 147.

[12]Albert C. Sundberg, Jr., "The Protestant Old Testament Canon: Should It Be Re-Examined?" *Catholic Biblical Quarterly* 28 (1966): 194-203. Cf. also Sundberg's "The Old Testament: A Christian Canon," cited above.

consequences of such decontextualization when, assuming a negative answer, he asks, "What claim does a doctrine of canon arising in Judaism following A.D. 70 have upon the doctrine of canon in the church?"[13]

Sundberg's sharp distinction between Scripture and canon rests upon dubious historical ground. S. J. P. K. Riekert points out that, "Sundberg's thesis that the third division of the canon had no limits before Jamnia is contradicted by Josephus' explicit testimony."[14] The passage in Josephus to which Riekert refers is *Contra Apionem* I. 37-43, which argues for a closed canon of twenty-two (rather than the traditional twenty-four) books.[15] The following excerpts from this passage point out the difficulty in maintaining a sharp distinction between Scripture and canon, which views the latter as only a late-developing notion.

> We do not possess myriads of inconsistent books, conflicting with each other. Our books, those which are justly accredited, are but two and twenty, and contain the record of all time. . . . We have given practical proof of our reverence for our own Scriptures. For, although such long ages have now passed, no one has ventured either to add, or to remove, or to alter a syllable; and it is an instinct with every Jew, from the day of his birth, to regard them as decrees of God, to abide by them, and, if need be, cheerfully to die for them. Time and again ere now the sight has been witnessed of prisoners enduring tortures and death in every form in the theatres, rather than utter a single word against the laws and the allied documents.[16]

Thus, Riekert seems correct when he observes that, "Documentary evidence compels one to reject the sharp distinction between Scripture and canon."[17]

---

[13]"The Protestant Old Testament Canon," 203.

[14]S. J. P. K. Riekert, "Critical Research and the One Christian Canon Comprising Two Testaments," in *The Relationship Between the Old and New Testament*, Neotestamentica 14, Proceedings of the Sixteenth Meeting of the New Testament Society of South Africa (n.p., 1980) 21-41, at 36.

[15]Josephus, *Contra Apionem/Against Apion*, trans. H. St. J. Thackeray, Loeb Classical Library (Cambridge MA: Harvard Univ. Press, 1961). The passage cited is found on 176-81.

[16]Ibid., I 38, 42-43.

[17]Riekert, "Critical Research," 21.

In Childs' approach, the relationship between Scripture and canon is more complex than that of Sundberg in two ways. First, the term canon is used to refer to the entire historical and theological process of the Jewish and Christian communities' recognition and reading of certain books as Scripture. Canon does not simply refer to the "final stages" of the process (the canonization of Scripture). As John Barton, who has been critical of Childs' approach, admits:

> If the word "canon" is to be used at all, then it should probably be in the sense in which the term was sometimes used in the early Church, to denote a "norm" or regulative standard rather than a closed body of texts.[18]

Second, even if one assumes a more restricted view of canon as canonization (the final boundary-fixing phase of the formation of Scripture), the historical evidence seems to indicate a much more fluid relationship between canonization and Scripture, rather than the sharp distinction ("closed collection") Sundberg claims.

James Barr specifically challenges Childs' definition of canon. Barr asserts that "*Canon* in this book [*Introduction to the Old Testament as Scripture*] is vaguely and unanalytically treated."[19] In a response to Barr, Childs defends his use of canon in the following fashion:

> I chose the term "canon" because it includes both the concepts of authority and reception in order to express the process and effect of this transmitting of religious traditions by a community of faith toward a certain end in all its various aspects. . . . I feel it is important to retain the term "canon" to emphasize that the process of religious interpretation by a historical faith community left its mark on a literary text which did not continue to evolve and which became the normative interpretation of those events to which it bore witness. Moreover, the term

---

[18]John Barton, *Oracles of God: Perceptions of Ancient Prophecy in Israel after the Exile* (New York: Oxford University Press, 1986) 63.

[19]James Barr, "Childs' *Introduction to the Old Testament as Scripture*," in *Journal for the Study of the Old Testament* 16 (1980) 12-23, at 13. For an expanded version of this criticism, see Barr's *Holy Scripture: Canon, Authority, Criticism.*

guards the factuality of a sacred text and does not allow it to be replaced by a mode of consciousness.[20]

In an effort to clarify conceptually his use of the term "canon," Childs uses Wittgenstein's model of language games, which we examined at the end of the last chapter. Childs explains his approach as follows:

> I am attempting to describe one "language game," namely the use of the Old Testament as scripture by a community of faith and practice. Expressed theologically, I am trying to explore how one reads the O.T. from a rule-of-faith called canon.[21]

Childs employs the term canon to describe the practices of communities of Jews and Christians, who have recognized and read the books of the Bible as normative. Such theological usage is not a one-time decision, but develops as a historical process in the life of communities of faith. In a response to critics of his Old Testament introduction, Childs describes his definition of canon as

> broadening the term canon to encompass the complex process involved in the religious usage of tradition which extended far back in Israel's history and exerted an increasing force in the post-exilic period.[22]

Childs uses the term canon without the article to signal this broader usage.[23]

Having examined Childs' definition of canon, we next explore his emphasis upon the final form of the biblical text, as we continue our description of his canonical approach.

---

[20]Brevard S. Childs, review of *Holy Scripture: Canon, Authority, Criticism*, by James Barr, *Interpretation*, 38 (1984): 66-70, at 68.

[21]Brevard S. Childs, "Response to Reviewers of *Introduction to the Old Testament as Scripture*," *Journal for the Study of the Old Testament* 16 (1980) 52-60, at 52.

[22]Ibid., 53.

[23]Ibid.

The Final Form of the Text

Childs' canonical approach focuses upon the text of Scripture, rather than upon any historical, philosophical, or literary concepts that seek to mediate between the biblical books and the communities of faith that read them as Scripture. Childs is specifically concerned with the final forms of the biblical books, which have been recognized as authoritative for the Jewish and Christian faith communities. Childs describes his focus upon the text's final form as follows:

> Canonical analysis focuses its attention on the effect which the different layers have had on the final form of the text, rather than using the text as a source for other information obtained by means of an oblique reading, such as the editor's self-understanding. A major warrant for this approach is found within the biblical tradition itself. The tradents have consistently sought to hide their own footprints in order to focus attention on the canonical text itself rather than the process.[24]

This emphasis upon the final form of the text is the most controversial aspect of Childs' approach.[25] Why does Childs develop this focus? What is so important about the final form of the text that one should distinguish it from all of the multitude of earlier, diverse forms of the traditions collected in the Scriptures of the Jewish and Christian communities?

For Childs, the answer to these questions is both historical and theological. The final forms of the biblical books are historically those forms of the literature that the Jewish and Christian communities have received and read as canonical Scripture for centuries. The final forms of the biblical books are theologically those forms of the literature where the communities claim to find the normative witness to God's revelation. Childs describes this

---

[24]Childs, "Exegetical Significance of Canon," 68.

[25]A detailed survey of the critical scholarly response is offered in chapter 3 of my "Canonical Hermeneutics." Beyond rhetorical concerns about the "rigidity" of Childs' emphasis, the discussion tends to fall into three patterns: (1) traditional historical-critical arguments, (2) new literary-critical questions (e.g., New Criticism, structuralism), and (3) theological concerns about the connection between authority and the final form of the text.

intersection between the historical and theological dimensions of Scripture in his article examining "The Canonical Shape of the Prophetic Literature."

> The significance of the final form of the biblical literature is that it alone bears witness to the full history of revelation. Within the Old Testament neither the process of its formation nor the history of its canonization is assigned an independent category. These dimensions have been either lost or purposely blurred. Rather, canon asserts that the witness to Israel's experience with God is testified to in the effect of the biblical text itself. It is only in the final form of the biblical text in which the normative history has reached an end that the full effect of this revelatory history can be perceived.[26]

I have elsewhere argued at length that the hermeneutics of Karl Barth provides the appropriate theological context for understanding Childs' canonical approach.[27] Barth's postcritical exegesis with its focus on the exact words of the biblical text clearly foreshadows Childs' emphasis upon the final form of the text. As Barth declares, exegesis must "allow even the detailed words of the text to speak exactly as they stand."[28] The canonical text of Scripture becomes the norm for biblical interpretation—i.e., the beginning and ending point of exegesis.[29] Even so vocal a critic of Barth's exegesis as James Barr admits,

> He [Barth] is quite right in arguing, as he often does, that theological exegesis should work from the text as it is. It is the given form of the

---

[26]Childs, "The Canonical Shape of Prophetic Literature," 47-48.

[27]See my "Canonical Hermeneutics," especially chap. 2. Also, a revised and abbreviated version of this material has been presented in a paper delivered at Regent's Park College, Oxford, entitled "Canonical Hermeneutics: Childs and Barth," which will be forthcoming in the *Scottish Journal of Theology*.

[28]The German original reads: "*die Texte genau zu Worte kommen lassen, wie sie lauten*" (Karl Barth, *Die Kirchliche Dogmatik*, [hereafter *K.D.*] 13 vols. and index vol. [Zollikon: Verlag der Evangelischen Buchhandlung, 1932-1970], I/2: 814). The English translation is *Church Dogmatics*, (hereafter *C.D.*) trans. Geoffrey Bromiley, *et al.* (Edinburgh: T. and T. Clark, 1955-1977), I/2: 726.

[29]For an example of Barth's emphasis on the canonical form of the text, which utilizes but finally subordinates historical-critical distinctions, see his theological exegesis of Numbers 13-14 (*K.D.*, IV/2:, 541-42; *C.D.*, IV/2: 478-79).

text, rather than the historical reorganization which we make by using the text as data, which provides the main content for our exegesis.[30]

A major consequence of this focus on the final form of the text, both for Childs and Barth, is the re-establishment post-critically of continuity with the entire historical tradition of exegesis, both "pre-critical" and critical. For example, Childs demonstrates a heightened appreciation of the role of midrash in the history of exegesis.[31] As he explains,

> Midrash is, above all, an interpretation of a canonical *text* within the context and for the religious purposes of a community, and is not just embellishment of tradition.[32]

Midrash is particularly important for understanding Childs' emphasis upon the final form of the text because it illustrates historically the dynamic of interpretation between a fixed text and a changing contemporary situation. Of course, this is not to say that Childs' canonical approach is simply a form of modern midrash; Childs' use of tradition history and other historical-critical methods rules out the danger of any such anachronistic attempt to repristinate traditional interpretation. Instead, the significance of midrash for Childs' approach lies in the way midrash demonstrates the dialectical interplay that exists between a canonical text and the situation of present faith communities for whom this text functions as canon. Childs offers the following description of the midrashic hermeneutical circle:

---

[30]Barr, *Old and New in Interpretation*, 93. Barr seeks to downplay this theme from his earlier writing in his later critique of Childs' approach.

[31]Renée Bloch, in a classic article on midrash and biblical interpretation, offers a useful definition of midrash as "an edifying and explanatory genre, in which the role of amplification is real but secondary and always remains subordinate to the primary religious end, which is to show the full import of the work of God, the Word of God" ("Midrash," trans. Mary Howard Callaway, in *Approaches to Ancient Judaism: Theory and Practice*, ed. William Scott Green [Missoula MT: Scholars Press, 1978] 29-50, at 29.

[32]Brevard S. Childs, "Midrash and the Old Testament," in *Understanding the Sacred Text: Essays in Honor of Morton S. Enslin on the Hebrew Bible and Christian Beginnings*, ed. J. Reumann (Valley Forge PA: Judson Press, 1972) 49.

The heart of the midrashic method is that the interpretation moves from the biblical text to seek a connection with a new situation. But then again, the reverse direction is equally important; namely, the interpretation comes from the situation and moves back to the text. In the first instance, the text interprets the new situation; in the second, the new situation illuminates the text.[33]

Thus, through an emphasis upon the final form of the text, Childs seeks to connect the interpretation of the Bible with its theological use as canon by both historical and contemporary communities of faith. Postcritical canonical hermeneutics seeks to maintain continuity with both "precritical" and critical traditions of exegesis.

Having examined Childs' controversial focus on the final form of the text, a brief discussion of the concept of the canonical shape of Scripture concludes our description of his canonical approach.

The Canonical Shape of Scripture

The canonical shape of Scripture is a theological *Gestalt*. The canon of Scripture functions wholistically as a written witness to the word and work of God. As Childs contends,

The concept of canon implies that the normative role of this Scripture functions through the shape which the church has given the tradition in its written form as a faithful witness to the redemptive work of God.[34]

As early as the publication in 1960 of *Myth and Reality in the Old Testament*, Childs asserted that the "new Israel" is theologically the "new reality" of the Old Testament, which only finds its fulfillment in the New Testament.[35] From his Christian confessional perspective, Childs maintained that the two testaments belong together.

---

[33]Ibid., 52.

[34]Brevard S. Childs, "The Old Testament as Scripture of the Church," *Concordia Theological Monthly* 43 (1972): 709-22, at 714.

[35]Studies in Biblical Theology 27 (Naperville IL: Alec R. Allenson; also London: SCM Press).

The Old Testament conceived of the experiences of Israel as the process by which God brought into being a new form of existence. . . . However, the Old Testament is also a history of Israel's rejection of the new way of life. . . . Because of the inability of the new existence to maintain itself within Israel, the Old Testament is theologically meaningless apart from the New Testament.[36]

Childs later extended and modified this view to include a specifically christocentric focus. For example, in his exegetical work on Psalm 8, Childs maintains that an adequate Christian theological interpretation of the psalm must be christological. As he argues,

From the point of view of Christian theology, it seems to me highly dubious that one can speak meaningfully of man and his relationship to God and the creation without speaking christologically. This position is not a simplistic christomonism, but a theological conviction held in common by Christian theologians from Augustine to Calvin, and beyond.[37]

The canonical shape of the text does not, of course, imply that there is one definitive interpretation for any given passage of Scripture. Rather, within the context of the canon there is a wide latitude for what contemporary literary critics have characterized as reader competence, reader response, or reception. As Childs explains in response to the criticisms of James Barr,

I do not wish to suggest that the canonical shaping provides a full-blown hermeneutic as if there were only one correct interpretation built into every text which a proper canonical reading could always recover. The canonical shaping provided larger contexts for interpretation, established the semantic level, and left important structural and material keys for understanding. Nevertheless, exegesis also involves the activity of the interpreter who from his modern context must also construe the material. There is an important dimension of "reader competence" which reacts to the coercion exercised by the text itself.[38]

---

[36]Childs, *Myth and Reality*, 97.

[37]Brevard S. Childs, "Psalm 8 in the Context of the Christian Canon," *Interpretation* 23 (1969): 20-31, at 26-27. This material was also published as one of Childs' exegetical tests of his method in *Biblical Theology in Crisis*, 151-163.

[38]Childs, review of *Holy Scripture: Canon, Authority, Criticism*, by James Barr, 69.

Childs contends that it is precisely the canonical shape of Scripture that has been ignored by historical-critical interpretation. This has resulted in an atomization of the canonical text, leading to a practical "decanonization" of Scripture. As Childs declares,

> The modern hermeneutical impasse has arisen in large measure by disregarding the canonical shaping. The usual critical methodology of restoring an original historical setting often involves stripping away the very elements which constitute the canonical shape. Little wonder that once the text has been anchored in the historical past by "decanonizing" it, the interpreter has difficulty applying it to a modern religious context![39]

Therefore, the hermeneutical dilemma of historical criticism provides the point of departure for Childs' efforts to develop his canonical approach. One must remember that Childs himself was an outstanding practitioner of form and tradition criticism during the early years of his career. Childs' work in this area was precisely what led to his conviction that "there was something fundamentally wrong with the foundations of the biblical discipline."[40]

Childs utilizes the following creative analogy to describe the situation to which his canonical approach is addressed:

> The issue at stake can be illustrated by another medium. Many of Hollywood's movies on biblical subjects—several of Cecil B. DeMille's productions come to mind—seem to reflect the latest historical knowledge on ancient Hebrew clothing, housing, and even language, but then miss the main point of the story. . . . It is simply not the case that the more historical and literary knowledge acquired, the better one is able to understand the biblical text. . . . Rather the issue turns on the use of

---

[39]Childs, "The Canonical Shape of the Prophetic Literature," 49.

[40]Childs, *IOTS*, 15. Childs further asserts, "I am now convinced that the relation between the historical critical study of the Bible and its theological use as religious literature within a community needs to be completely rethought. Minor adjustments are not only inadequate, but also conceal the extent of the dry rot" (ibid.)

proper discernment. How does one wisely use historical-critical tools in illuminating the canonical text?[41]

We have considered Childs' canonical approach to biblical interpretation in some detail, focusing upon his definition of canon, the controversial emphasis upon the final form of the text, and the theological concept of the canonical shape of Scripture. Now, in order to assist our understanding of Childs' approach, we turn to the question of application. What do all of these hermeneutical concepts look like in action? To respond to this question, we briefly survey some examples of Childs' exegesis in the context of the Christian canon.

· Exegetical Examples ·

The final test of any theory of biblical interpretation is the concrete one of its application to the exegesis of specific texts. In the case of Childs' canonical approach, with its emphasis upon the canonical shaping of biblical books, it is particularly at the level of interpreting larger contexts such as whole books and other major sections of Scripture that the most distinctive results are obtained.

The three examples that we examine have been carefully chosen to exhibit a range of the major themes and some of the diversity in Childs' exegetical work. Selected quotations from Childs' writings provide a sense of his style of interpretation. We will begin with the book of Deuteronomy, which was pivotal for the early development of Childs' approach.

Deuteronomy

As Childs engaged in the form critical and tradition historical work for his second major publication, *Memory and Tradition in Israel* (1962), his study of the book of Deuteronomy already began to raise questions about the problem of relating biblical traditions

---

[41]Brevard S. Childs, "On Reading the Elijah Narratives," *Interpretation* 34 (1980): 128-37, at 129-30.

to future generations.[42] Here in embryonic form one finds the sort of theological concerns that resulted in Childs' concept of the canonical shaping of biblical books. For instance, Childs described the "theological development" of Deuteronomy's usage of *zkr* ("remember") in the following way:

> The writer has as his chief problem the relating of the new generation of Israel to the tradition of Moses. No longer has Israel direct access to the redemptive events of the past. Now memory takes on central theological significance. Present Israel has not been cut off from redemptive history, but she encounters the same covenant God through a living tradition. Memory provides the link between past and present.[43]

A decade later, in his article "The Old Testament as Scripture of the Church" (1972), one discovers that Childs had developed and labeled the concept of canonical shaping and was beginning to explore its theological implications. The following exegetical analysis of the book of Deuteronomy provides a good illustration of Childs' application of his newly developed canonical approach.

> The book consists of a series of speeches by Moses to the people in which he explains and recapitulates the meaning of the Sinai law. Moreover, the setting is on the plains of Moab just before Israel is poised to enter the promised land. Moses addresses a new generation of Israelites, the older generation who had experienced the original covenant ceremony having died through disobedience. Therefore, right from the outset, one senses that the Book of Deuteronomy bears the explicit role through its canonical shaping of reinterpreting the events of Sinai for future generations. . . . First of all the writer makes clear in his homily that the original covenant concerned the later generations of Israel as much as the first. . . . Secondly, the interpretation of Moses is future-oriented. . . . Thirdly, the purpose of Deuteronomy is to inculcate the law in the heart of the people. . . . Finally, the author offers a profound theological reflection on the meaning of election lest Israel misunderstand what is her responsibility as the chosen people.[44]

---

[42]Brevard S. Childs, *memory and Tradition in Israel*, Studies in Biblical Theology 37 (Naperville IL: Alec R. Allenson, 1962; also London: SCM Press, 1962).

[43]Childs, *Memory and Tradition*, 72.

[44]Childs, "The Old Testament as Scripture of the Church," 720.

The process of Childs' development of a canonical interpretation of the book of Deuteronomy reached it final stage with
the publication in 1979 of his *Introduction to the Old Testament as
Scripture*. Particularly in Childs' discussion of "the structure and
style of the book as a whole," one sees the mature exposition of his
proposal.

> The canonical approach does not deny that forces from Deuteronomy's
> early history have left a stamp on the material, such as liturgical patterns
> from the cult (von Rad) or a common ancient Near Eastern treaty
> structure (Baltzer). However, the point of debate lies in determining how
> these earlier levels now function within the context of a canonical collec-
> tion of sacred scripture. . . . Moses explains the law book by
> recapitulating what has happened as well as applying the divine law to
> the new situation in which the people would shortly enter. It is, there-
> fore, built into the canonical function of Deuteronomy that a new
> application of old tradition is being offered, but a tradition which had
> already assumed a normative, written form. The homiletical style which
> belongs to the present shape of the book is an essential part of the
> explanation of the law. The new interpretation seeks to actualize the
> traditions of the past for the new generation in such a way as to evoke
> a response of the will in a fresh commitment to the covenant. The pre-
> sent form of the book of Deuteronomy reflects a dominant editorial
> concern to reshape the material for its use by future generations of Israel.
> The process can be termed canonical because it relates to the use of
> tradition as authoritative scripture rather than by initiating a liturgical
> actualization or legitimating a process of continuous reinterpretation.[45]

Childs' exegesis of the book of Deuteronomy thus provides
both a window on the process of his early development of the concept of the canonical shaping of biblical books and a clear model
of the mature application of his canonical approach.

Exodus

Childs' exegetical work on the book of Exodus, which culminated
in a major commentary published in 1974, provides a full-scale
example of the application of his canonical approach to the

---

[45]Childs, *IOTS*, 211-12.

interpretation of a complex biblical book.[46] The organization of the commentary itself—beginning each section with detailed textual and tradition historical discussion and moving in concentric circles through wider contexts of interpretation and theological reflection —models the various levels of meaning encompassed by the canonical approach.

At the outset of the commentary Childs makes explicit the theological dimensions of the project.

> The purpose of this commentary is unabashedly theological. Its concern is to understand Exodus as scripture of the church. The exegesis arises as a theological discipline within the context of the canon and is directed toward the community of faith which lives by its confession of Jesus Christ.

. . . .

> The aim of this commentary is to seek to interpret the book of Exodus as canonical scripture within the theological discipline of the Christian church. . . . The author does not share the hermeneutical position of those who suggest that biblical exegesis is an objective, descriptive enterprise, controlled solely by scientific criticism, to which the Christian theologian can at best add a few homiletical reflections for piety's sake. In my judgment, the rigid separation between the descriptive and constructive elements of exegesis strikes at the roots of the theological task of understanding the Bible.[47]

During his preparation of the commentary, Childs offered a three-point summary of his view of the canonical shape of the book and its theological implications in an article:

> [1] A basic feature of the Book of Exodus is the interchange of narrative and legal material. The narrative material testifies to the historical moment at a particular time in Israel's history at which God made His will known to His people. . . . Conversely, the legal formulations made evident that his covenant rested upon commandments which could be clearly understood and followed. . . . In the canonical form the two

---

[46]*The Book of Exodus: A Critical, Theological Commentary*, The Old Testament Library (Philadelphia: Westminster Press, 1974; also London: SCM Press, 1974, under the title *Exodus, A Commentary*).

[47]Ibid., ix, xiii.

elements belong together, inextricably bound. Gospel and Law cannot be divorced.

[2] The Book of Exodus has often combined the account of an original event with an account of the ongoing celebration of that same event. The intertwining of the original passover with the later observance of the rite is a prime example of this practice. . . . [This provides] a channel of appropriation for every future generation.

[3] It is theologically significant to note that the Sinai material has been edited in such a way that the covenant is both preceded and followed by stories of Israel's murmuring and resistance to the law of God. . . . [The story of the Golden Calf shows] how the demands of God upon His people are continually supported by His mercy in the light of repeated disobedience and even apostasy.[48]

The influence of Karl Barth upon Childs' theological interpretation of Exodus becomes clearly apparent in the refusal finally to separate "word and event." As Childs maintains,

The biblical writer brackets the Exodus event with a preceding and a succeeding interpretation. He does not see the Exodus as an "act of God" distinct from the "word of God" which explains it. In theological terms, the relation between act and interpretation, or event and word, is one which cannot be separated.[49]

Childs defines two areas of "common ground" between the canonical witness to an event and extra-biblical evidence. First, "the canonical witness shares all the features common to human language."[50] Second, in a fashion reminiscent of Barth's doctrine of Scripture ("the Word of God in the words of men"),

the area of common ground between the canonical witness and the extra-biblical extends to the content of both in all its aspects. The two share thought patterns, institutions, and experiences of ordinary human life. . . . The canonical writings function as God's vehicle specifically in its human form. There is no way to extract the purely "divine" elements.[51]

---

[48]"The Old Testament as Scripture of the Church," 719.
[49]Childs, *Exodus*, 204.
[50]Ibid., 301.
[51]Ibid.

Childs' interpretation of the Exodus narrative itself reveals the conscious subordination of historical-critical research to a canonical reading of the final form of the text. This subordination includes Childs' own substantial and creative tradition historical work on this narrative.[52] As he explains,

> It is a source of frustration common to most readers of commentaries that so much energy is spent on the analysis of the prehistory of a text as to leave little for a treatment of the passage in its final form. The complaint is certainly justified. Ultimately the use of source and form criticism is exegetically deficient if these tools do not illuminate the canonical text.[53]

Childs views the recovery of earlier forms of the text through historical-critical scholarship as offering a "depth dimension" that serves to illuminate the interpretation of the final form of the text. As he observes in commenting on the theophany at Sinai in Exodus 19-20,

> There is great need not to allow evidence from the earlier development of the text to undercut dealing seriously with the final stage of the text. This does not mean that the modern exegete can operate with the present text midrashically. . . . One must be aware of a depth dimension and of a variety of forces which have been at work, while at the same time concentrating one's efforts in interpreting the biblical text before one.[54]

Our examination of some features of Childs' exegesis of the books of Deuteronomy and Exodus has illustrated the operation of his canonical approach to biblical interpretation in the area where it was first developed. For our final exegetical example we turn to Childs' extension of his approach to the books of the New Testament and examine briefly his exegesis of Ephesians.

---

[52]For example, Brevard S. Childs, "A Traditio-historical Study of the Reed Sea Tradition," *Vetus Testamentum* 20 (1970): 406-18.

[53]Childs, *Exodus*, 149.

[54]Ibid., 364-65.

Ephesians

Because of its highly theological character, the letter to the Ephesians sharply raises the hermeneutical issue of the connection
between historical interpretation and theological reflection. Childs'
exegesis rejects a sharp dichotomy between a supposedly objective
task of historical description and a later subjective activity of practical application. Instead, a canonical approach offers a more
hermeneutically interwoven treatment of the exegetical task. Childs
offers the following overview of these hermeneutical concerns in
his discussion of Ephesians:

> Basic hermeneutical issues are at stake as to how one approaches the
> biblical text. I disagree with those who feel that the appeal to the
> modern reader is simply a pious convention, left over from a past un-
> critical era, and more suitable for homilists than exegetes. Nor do I feel
> that the theological issue involved is to be restricted to a final stage of
> reflection, as if the question of the modern addressee could only prop-
> erly be raised after the solid, objective task of historical interpretation
> had been completed. Rather, it seems to me an essential part of the
> descriptive task to seek to understand how this ancient letter was trans-
> mitted, shaped, and interpreted in order to render its message accessible
> to successive generations of believers by whom and for whom it was
> treasured as authoritative.[55]

A crucial issue differentiating a canonical approach to Ephesians from representative historical-critical discussions is the status
given to the relationship between the historical Paul and the book.
So much scholarly ink has been spilled over the question of Pauline authorship of the book that this issue has tended to dominate
the discussion of both liberal and conservative exegetes. It is as if
the theological validity of the book turns on the demonstration of
the historical identity of its author. Childs argues that this state of
affairs ignores the significance of the "canonical Paul" in understanding the role of Ephesians in the New Testament.

> Most critical scholars seem to assume that first one constructs a profile
> of the "historical Paul," and then one determines to what extent one can

---

[55]Childs, *NTAC*, 322-23.

or cannot include Ephesians within Pauline theology. . . . In my opinion, such an approach has turned the purpose of the New Testament canon on its head and badly misconstrued its theological function. The primary issue is not whether or not Ephesians is Pauline. The canonical process has already incorporated it within the Pauline corpus. Rather, the exegetical issue is to determine the effect which the inclusion of the letter has on its shape and on the understanding of the corpus. The canonical decision has rendered a theological judgment as to what constitutes the "canonical Paul." Although it remains a valid and important question to consider the relationship between the "canonical" and the "historical" Paul, the two entities cannot be identified, nor can the latter determination establish the parameters of the former. The function of the canon is to establish the shape of the vehicle to which the true Pauline witness to the gospel is made.[56]

Given this canonical reorientation of the interpretation of the book, what is the book's theological significance? What is the connection between the canonical shape of Ephesians and its theological function for generations of Christians who regard it as Scripture? Childs' response to these questions points to a dynamic canonical process that transforms the original forms of the literature into Scripture functioning as theological reflection, witness, and praise. Childs summarizes the process and its effects as follows:

Our study of the canonical process of shaping the Pauline corpus has sought to demonstrate that the form-critical distinction between an occasional letter and a theological tractate has been increasingly blurred. The effect has been to subordinate the different original forms of literature into vehicles for suitable theological witness. Whether one regards Ephesians as a letter or theological tractate is unimportant as long as these terms are given their content by the literature's actual function. In a real sense, Ephesians establishes a true canonical model for defining the nature of genuine theological reflection. Far from its being a detached, abstract exercise, the letter establishes the liturgical context for divine praise in theological reflection which moves from the indicatives of the gospel to concrete implications for Christian living in the world and which is grounded in God's present activity on behalf of his creation.[57]

---

[56]Ibid., 323.
[57]Ibid., 324-25.

Thus, Childs' canonical approach to Ephesians takes seriously the historical questions of the epistle's authorship and original form, but does not regard these concerns as the center of exegesis. Instead, these matters are subordinated to an interpretive focus upon the epistle's actual function as part of the Scripture of Christian faith communities. The canonical process is a dynamic shaping and religious construal of the epistle, which reflects its various roles in the life of those communities that have read and preserved it as normative.

We have surveyed some highlights of Childs' exegesis of the books of Deuteronomy, Exodus, and Ephesians, in order to provide some concrete examples of Childs' canonical approach in operation. We next consider some modifications of Childs' approach, in response to four important criticisms that it has received.

· Criticisms and Modifications ·

Amongst the many criticisms of Childs' canonical approach offered by scholars in the widespread discussion that followed his proposal, four are of particular significance.[58] These criticisms not only seem justified, but call for some alteration in Childs' understanding of canonical hermeneutics. Each of the four criticisms is described briefly, followed by my suggestions for modifications of the canonical approach in response.

The Deuterocanonical Books

Childs' Old Testament introduction, in typical Protestant fashion, does not include any treatment of the so-called "apocryphal" books of the Old Testament. Instead, Childs maintains that the final limits of the Jewish canon should be observed by Christian interpreters. Childs acknowledges that "Jewish and Christian groups . . . continued to use non-canonical books with varying degrees of authority."[59] Nevertheless, he maintains that,

---

[58]See note 1 for my survey of international response to Childs' proposal.
[59]Childs, *IOTS*, 67.

The canonization process within Judaism thus involved a selection of a limited number of books from a much larger resource of available literature. . . . the effect of the exclusion of the apocryphal and pseudepigraphical books can be clearly recognized in the subsequent history of Judaism.[60]

For Childs this authority of the Jewish canon is linked to the authority of the Hebrew text. He particularly singles out the emergence of the Masoretic text as "the *vehicle* both for recovering and for understanding the canonical text of the Old Testament."[61] Childs argues for this choice on two different grounds. The first is the pragmatic one that only the Jewish community that supported the Masoretic text survived historically "as the living vehicle of the whole canon of Hebrew scripture."[62]

The weakness of this argument lies in its equation of historical dominance with the theological determination of the boundaries of "the whole canon." Applied to the history of the early church, it would seem to argue for the inclusion of the deuterocanonical books, rather than their exclusion.

Childs' second ground of argument for the Masoretic text is a text critical one. He claims that,

The increasing authority of the Masoretic text among the Greek-speaking Jews of the Hellenistic period who used a translated form of their Bible is clearly evident in the recensional history of the Septuagint. From the Jewish perspective the Greek Bible never had an independent integrity which could contest the Hebrew. Thus the Greek was continually brought into conformity with the Hebrew and never the reverse.[63]

Kevin O'Connell points out the weakness of this argument for the support of Childs' claims regarding the Masoretic text:

Since various distinct Hebrew versions are available in the first centuries B.C. and A.D., and since more than one version served as the target for

---

[60]Ibid., 66-67.

[61]Ibid., 97.

[62]Ibid. Childs acknowledges the survival of the Samaritan community but points to its sectarian position as resulting from its recognition of "only a portion of the total Hebrew scriptures" (98).

[63]Ibid., 98-99.

Greek recensional activity, it remains difficult to absolutize the canonical authority of the Hebrew version ultimately chosen by the Jewish community.[64]

Given the difficulties in arguing for a single received text of the Hebrew Bible that is normative for Jews and Christians, it would seem wiser to adopt a more flexible view about the exact boundaries of the canon. Such a view would be based upon the actual continuing usage of specific books as authoritative Scripture by communities of faith. The patterns of reading and reception of certain books as sacred Scripture, rather than any historical claims regarding their authorship or apostolicity, constitute the criteria for canonicity. Thus, if generations of Christians have recognized a specific group of books as having secondary canonical status, canonical hermeneutics should be able to recognize and evaluate this claim, rather than simply excluding it by dubious historical and textual arguments, which reflect confessional differences.

In the case of the deuterocanonical books, one must admit that the Reformers' ambivalent relationship to the early traditions of the Western church plays a major role in the attitude of Protestant theology to this question.[65] This ambivalence may perhaps best be epitomized in Calvin's extensive appropriation of Augustine's biblical interpretation, while rejecting Augustine's conclusions concerning the deuterocanonical books.[66]

A less rigid specification of the exact boundaries of canon would more accurately reflect the complex and diverse historical process of canon formation. Furthermore, acknowledgement of the legitimacy of claims of other Christians to include the deuterocanonical books would encourage less polemical disputation

---

[64]Kevin G. O'Connell, review of Childs, *IOTS*, *Biblical Archaeologist* 44 (1981): 187-88, at 188.

[65]For further discussion of this issue from a Protestant perspective see Marvin E. Tate, "The Old Testament Apocrypha and the Old Testament Canon," *Review and Expositor* 65 (1968): 339-56.

[66]See, for example, *Institutes*, III, 5, 8, and IV, 9, 14 (John Calvin, *Institutes of the Christian Religion*, 2 vols., ed. John T. McNeill, trans. Ford Lewis Battles [London: SCM Press, 1961] I: 678-79; II: 1178-79).

regarding their status and more critical examination regarding their usefulness.

The Hermeneutical Notion of Tradition

Much of Childs' understanding of tradition derives from his training and early work as an historical-critical exegete.[67] According to this method, the goal of exegesis is to seek to reconstruct critically the original traditions behind the text. As Childs shifted his focus to the hermeneutical issues surrounding the concept of canon, his idea of tradition still remained largely concerned with the reconstruction of the prehistory of the text. For example, a reader of Childs' Old and New Testament introductions cannot help but notice how preoccupied Childs seems with the detailed rehearsal and evaluation of the historical-critical state of the question against which his canonical proposal is set. At times the focus upon the historical-critical reconstruction of tradition is so great as to outweigh Childs' efforts to specify both the canonical shape of a biblical book and its larger theological and hermeneutical implications.[68] Childs' concept of tradition is overburdened by his historical-critical inheritance.

This inadequacy of Childs' understanding of tradition could be remedied by a selective appropriation of Hans-Georg Gadamer's hermeneutical notion of tradition. The examination of Gadamer's work on tradition and language in the previous chapter described Gadamer's dialogical model of tradition, which dynamically encompasses the entire history of the text and its effects upon its interpreters.[69] For Gadamer, the meaning of a classic text like the Bible is an ever-changing process (commonly labeled a "fusion of horizons"), which unites historical study of the prehistory of the

---

[67]See especially Childs' second major work, *Memory and Tradition in Israel.*

[68]Childs' exegesis of the book of Esther (*IOTS*, 598-607) provides a clear and concise example of this tendency. Following a wide-ranging summary of historical critical problems, the canonical shaping of the book is limited to a brief discussion of the function of the appendix (9:20-32) and the typifying of characters. Theological and hermeneutical implications of the book are reduced to a three-paragraph postscript to the discussion.

[69]See the section entitled "Tradition and Language—Gadamer" in Chapter 2.

text with all the levels of its appropriation as a living tradition, including the perspectives of contemporary communities of inter-preters.

The discussion of Gadamer's model argued that the appropria-tion of his hermeneutical notion of tradition does not necessarily entail the adoption of Gadamer's philosophical framework of ideal-istic ontology. Rather, his hermeneutical notion of tradition may be selectively appropriated for use in nonfoundationalist philosophical approaches like the postcritical categories of Wittgenstein. It is pre-cisely this *selective* nonfoundationalist appropriation of Gadamer's hermeneutical notion of tradition that I am advocating for canon-ical hermeneutics.

The adaptation of Gadamer's view to canonical hermeneutics offers two major benefits. First, Childs' inadequate concept of tradition is freed from its historical-critical limitations, as a meth-odological concept bound to the prehistory of the text.[70] Instead, tradition becomes a dynamic, text-centered concept, which encom-passes the entire history of interpretation. Second, Gadamer's emphasis upon community reinforces Childs' theme of the inter-pretation of the Bible as Scripture by communities of faith. Such a community-centered perspective offers a corrective to individual-istic notions of interpretation, which jeopardize postcritical models (e.g., the criticism of the absence of community in Wittgenstein's philosophy).

The Problem of Canonical Intentionality

Childs' notion of canonical intentionality has been sharply criti-cized as imprecise by various reviewers of his work.[71] In response to this criticism Childs has attempted to explain and defend his view as follows:

---

[70]Gadamer's critique of the hegemony of method would reduce Childs' preoc-cupation with historical-critical reconstruction.

[71]For a range of critical evaluations of Childs' proposal for a canonical ap-proach to Old Testament interpretation, see the essays collected in *Journal for the Study of the Old Testament* 16 (1980) and in *Horizons in Biblical Theology* 2 (1980).

> Regardless of the different levels of intentionality which were involved in the historical formulation of the material, the literature was received within a religious context and assigned an authoritative function by different communities of faith and practice. . . . a special level of intentionality was assigned to the literature as a whole by virtue of its accepted role as Scripture.[72]

Childs' advocacy of this special level of canonical intentionality seeks to move away from the old idea of authorial intentionality as the norm for interpretation and towards a text-grounded, hermeneutical construct. The status of the special level, however, is not precisely defined. It remains unclear how the notion of canonical intentionality is related to the process of reading the books of the Bible as Scripture. As Wittgenstein has observed, intention is inextricably tied to a larger socio-linguistic context.

> An intention is embedded in its situation, in human customs and institutions. If the technique of the game of chess did not exist, I could not intend to play a game of chess. In so far as I do intend the construction of a sentence in advance, that is made possible by the fact that I can speak the language in question.[73]

Childs' notion of canonical intentionality stands in need of clarification precisely at this point of its embeddedness in the larger socio-linguistic situation. In the second chapter Paul Ricoeur's dialectical theory of reading and his mimetic view of historical intentionality were discussed. Taken together these theories provide a way of linking canonical intentionality to the dynamics of the reading process itself. Ricoeur's understanding of the text as a "work" that results in "distantiation" from the author leads to a notion of textual intentionality.

Unfortunately, Childs has sought to differentiate sharply between his approach and Ricoeur's phenomenological hermeneutics. In his Old Testament introduction, Childs contends,

> In the philosophical hermeneutics of Paul Ricoeur and his followers the Bible is seen as a deposit of metaphors which contain inherent powers

---

[72]"A Response," *Horizons in Biblical Theology* 2 (1980): 199-211, at 206-207.
[73]*P.I.*, I: 337.

by which to interpret and order the present world of experience, regardless of the source of imagery. The concern is to illuminate what lies 'ahead' (*devant*) of the text, not behind. This approach shows little or no interest in the historical development of the biblical text or even in the historical context of the canonical text. The crucial interpretive context in which the metaphors function is provided by the faith community itself (cf. D. Kelsey [*The Uses of Scripture in Recent Theology*]).[74]

Childs' criticisms of Ricoeur fail to take into account the different perspective that results from Ricoeur's philosophical background and multi-disciplinary treatment of hermeneutics. Childs is simply incorrect in claiming that Ricoeur is uninterested in the matter of "historical context." Although Ricoeur is not pursuing a traditional historical investigation of the biblical text, his deep interest in the significance of history may be seen quite clearly and at length in the first volume of *Time and Narrative*. The issue is not that Ricoeur lacks interest in the historical context of Scripture. Rather, Ricoeur's cross-disciplinary philosophical hermeneutics approaches the biblical text with a different set of questions concerning its historical context than those generally pursued by biblical scholarship.[75]

Childs' approach maintains that canonicity changes "the original semantic level" of much of the biblical material, thus creating the special level of canonical intentionality. As Childs explains,

The canonical process often assigned a function to the literature as a whole which transcended its parts. The collection acquired a theological role in instructing, admonishing and edifying a community of faith, and that altered its original semantic level. Frequently a particular story was deemed paradigmatic of God's ways with his people.[76]

---

[74]Childs, *IOTS*, 77. David Kelsey, *The Uses of Scripture in Recent Theology* (Philadelphia: Fortress Press, 1975). Childs also cites Ricoeur's work on parable in *NTAC*, 532, and Ricoeur's work on evil in *OTT*, 91.

[75]For a good example of the sort of questions Ricoeur's approach raises for biblical scholarship, see his "Preface to Bultmann," trans. Peter McCormick, in *The Conflict of Interpretations*, 381-401, and reprinted in Paul Ricoeur, *Essays on Biblical Interpretation*, ed. Lewis S. Mudge (Philadelphia: Fortress Press, 1980) 49-72.

[76]Childs, *OTT*, 22-23.

Ricoeur's theory of reading offers a detailed description of how such a changed semantic level might occur. Since language is "composed of a hierarchy of levels," (moving from the level of the word to that of the sentence to that of discourse) exegesis within a canonical context could be understood as corresponding to a movement along this hierarchy.[77] Each succeeding context for interpretation in a critical, theological commentary like Childs' *Exodus*— beginning with the textual investigation of individual words and culminating in theological reflection in the context of the entire Christian canon throughout the history of exegesis—could thus be situated along a hermeneutical spectrum of meaning.

Given this picture of the interpretive process, then Childs' canonical intentionality, like Ricoeur's mimetic historical intentionality, works through the reading process to ground a larger vision by referring specifically to the narrative shape ("configuration") of the texts themselves. Therefore, canonical intentionality does not refer to the specific intentions of some historically-reconstructed author or editor of the texts. Nor does it refer to the subjective intentions of some historical agent behind the texts, whether personal (e.g., Moses) or structural (e.g., the priests, the Massoretes). Canonical intentionality refers to the theologically-construed shape ("configuration") of the texts themselves.

Thus, Childs' imprecise notion of canonical intentionality is clarified by locating it within Ricoeur's dialectical theory of reading and specifying its function using Ricoeur's mimetic view of historical intentionality.

We now turn to one other modification of Childs' approach in which Ricoeur's philosophical hermenutics will be of assistance— the need for greater inclusion of contemporary sociological and literary approaches to biblical interpretation.

The Incorporation of Sociological and Literary Approaches

A major weakness of Childs' proposal lies in its lack of openness to contemporary sociological and literary approaches to biblical interpretation. Even a cursory examination of any of Childs' major

---

[77]Ricoeur, "Structure, Word, Event," 80.

works reveals his intensive engagement with traditional historical-critical exegesis and a relatively minimal notice of other more recent critical approaches. Besides factors arising from Childs' own training and early work in traditio-historical criticism, an important theological concern seems to underlie Childs' lack of openness in this area.

Following Barth's rejection of anthropocentric theology, Childs is suspicious of any approach to biblical theology that does not emphasize the christological role of the Christian canon.[78] Childs seems afraid—and not without some historical warrant—that any hermeneutical approach that opens itself completely to human development, social psychological, and political perspectives will already have taken those first fateful steps down the primrose path that leads to Feuerbach.[79] Much of the philosophical dynamic that underlies such theological reductionism resides in the Hegelian drive to absolute knowledge. When the turn to the human subject is allied with the claim for absolute knowledge, it may be subverted into the deification of the human subject.

Ricoeur's hermeneutics of testimony provides a possible way of bypassing such theological reductionism. Ricoeur offers a phenomenological demonstration of the hermeneutical grounds for the rejection of Hegel's claim for absolute knowledge.[80] Ricoeur's hermeneutical critique signifies the end of transparent consciousness and transparent knowledge.

Ricoeur declares that only "a *critical* act" provides the means for a "finite consciousness" to "appropriate the affirmation which constitutes it."[81] Therefore, it is impossible for finite consciousness "to grasp both consciousness of the absolute and consciousness of

---

[78]An example of this continuing Barthian influence in Childs' work is provided by his essay, "Gerhard von Rad in American Dress," in *The Hermeneutical Quest: Essays in Honor of James Luther Mays on His Sixty-Fifth Birthday* (Allison Park PA: Pickwick Publications, 1986).

[79]For Barth's sketch of the "catastrophe" of the primrose path to Feuerbach, see *C.D.* I/2: 288-91.

[80]Paul Ricoeur, "The Hermeneutics of Testimony, " trans. David E. Stewart and Charles E. Regan, in Ricoeur, *Essays on Biblical Interpretation*, 119-54.

[81]Ibid., 146.

itself."[82] This means that a philosophy of consciousness, especially one that glorifies the human subject itself, becomes impossible.

Ricoeur's nuanced use of critical hermeneutics in his critique of Hegel results in two counterbalancing consequences. On the one hand, philosophical hermeneutics is delivered from its ideological captivity to idealistic ontology—a bondage for which Gadamer has been soundly criticized by Jürgen Habermas.[83] On the other hand, the "hermeneutics of suspicion" of Freud, Marx, Nietzsche, and their contemporary successors is employed heuristically but held in tension within the hermeneutical arc, which seeks to integrate explanation and understanding.[84] As we discussed in the second chapter, Ricoeur's hermeneutical arc provides a model for the process of reading as the recovery of meaning across diverse and often conflicting levels of interpretation.

Thus, the appropriation of Ricoeur's critique of Hegel in the context of Ricoeur's theory of reading as the recovery of meaning offers a way for a canonical approach to biblical interpretation to avoid the theological reductionism associated with both idealistic and critical approaches to hermeneutics. Canonical hermeneutics would be able to exhibit greater openness to the insights of critical sociological and literary studies of the Bible without fear of succumbing to reductionistic perspectives on Scripture.

This chapter has sought to describe Childs' canonical approach to biblical interpretation and to develop a carefully modified version of canonical hermeneutics in response to significant criticisms of its weaknesses. Proposed modifications have specifically addressed the issues of the place of the deuterocanonical books, the hermeneutical concept of tradition, the problem of canonical

---

[82]Ibid.

[83]Jürgen Habermas, "The Hermeneutic Claim to Universality," trans. Josef Bleicher, in *Contemporary Hermeneutics*, 181-211, especially 190-91.

[84]For further explanation of Ricoeur's analysis of the "hermeneutics of suspicion" see Ricoeur's article, "Psychoanalysis and the Movement of Contemporary Culture," trans. Willis Domingo in *The Conflict of Interpretations*, 121-59, especially 148-50. For a fuller treatment of this topic see Ricoeur's *Freud and Philosophy: An Essay on Interpretation*, trans. Denis Savage (New Haven: Yale University Press, 1970) particularly 32-36.

intentionality, and the incorporation of contemporary sociological and literary approaches to biblical interpretation.

Having developed this modified version of canonical hermeneutics, we explore in the next chapter its application to the task of shaping a postcritical evangelical theology.

CANONICAL HERMENEUTICS: POSTCRITICAL THEOLOGICAL PROLEGOMENA

How can the carefully nuanced understanding of canonical hermeneutics that we developed in the preceding chapter help us to do theology? In what ways can all of these rather technical modifications of Childs' canonical approach to biblical interpretation assist us to negotiate that treacherous and slippery divide between Scripture and doctrine?

In this chapter I seek to show that canonical hermeneutics can offer evangelical Christians some guidance in moving from biblical hermeneutics to a doctrine of Scripture. In particular, I think that canonical hermeneutics offers a way of bridging the great gap between traditional (often inaccurately labeled "precritical"[1]) biblical interpretation and historical-critical (more accurately labeled "European Enlightenment"[2]) biblical interpretation. This gap is an expression of the famous "ugly ditch" that Lessing found between "the accidental truths of history" and "the necessary truths of reason."[3]

---

[1]A number of scholars in the field of the history of exegesis have demonstrated the inadequacy of this label. Perhaps the most well-known of these efforts is David Steinmetz's provocative article, "The Superiority of Pre-Critical Exegesis," *Theology Today* 37 (1980): 27-38.

[2]Third-world scholars, particularly those with commitments to liberation theology, have been especially energetic in pointing out the social location of historical-critical scholarship. For a thoughtful, biblical approach that attempts to blend rather than polarize, see J. Severino Croatto, *Biblical Hermenutics: Toward a Theory of Reading as the Production of Meaning*, trans. Robert R. Barr (Maryknoll NY: Orbis, 1987).

[3]See especially Gotthold Ephraim Lessing, "On the Proof of the Spirit and of Power," (1777), in *Lessing's Theological Writings*, ed. Henry Chadwick (Stanford: Stanford University Press, 1956). Mark Brett offers a valuable historical discussion of this matter in relation to Childs in a chapter entitled, "Has Childs Fallen into Gabler's Ditch?," in Mark G. Brett, *Biblical Criticism in Crisis? The Impact of the Canonical Approach on Old Testament Studies* (Cambridge: Cambridge University Press, 1991) 76-115.

Thus, this chapter argues that a carefully nuanced canonical hermeneutics can provide the central theme for postcritical theological prolegomena. An evangelical doctrine of Scripture that utilizes a postcritical canonical hermeneutic to unite traditional and historical-critical approaches to biblical interpretation is the outcome of such reflection. To move toward this goal we briefly consider in turn the relationship of Scripture to doctrine, tradition, history, and pattern. At each point our concern is to discern the relationship between canonical hermeneutics and various aspects of the theological interpretation of Scripture.

· Scripture and Doctrine: Canon as the Rule of Scripture ·

When ancient Greek writers took the word referring to a "straight rod" (*kanōn*) and used it to describe a "rule or standard," the roots for a regulative understanding of this word were planted.[4] Then as second-century Christian exegetes, following the example of Philo, began to use "canon" in conjunction with "truth" to refer to God's revelation, the theological use of the term was established.[5] The close association of "canon" with the Latin *regula fidei* (rule of faith) gradually resulted in the identification of both of these terms with the emerging authoritative collections of writings that were to become the Jewish and Christian Scriptures.

Thus canon came to be seen as the rule that these particular books, rather than others, were to be read as Holy Scripture. For the Christian community this rule of canon reflected the experience of the church in the use of these books. When the books were read, Christians both discovered in them the Word of God and learned to hear them (and not others) as the Word of God. This dialectic

---

[4]For the standard lexicographical account of the word see H.G. Liddell, R. Scott, and H. S. Jones, *A Greek-English Lexicon* (Oxford: Clarendon Press, 1940), *ad loc.*, and W. F. Arndt and F. W. Gingrich, *A Greek-English Lexicon of the New Testament and Other Early Christian Literature* (Chicago: University of Chicago Press, 1957), *ad loc.* For further detailed discussion of the New Testament period usages, Theodore Zahn's work (as cited in Arndt and Gingrich) is especially important.

[5]Philo, *Legum Allegoriae*, 3, 233.

between God's speaking and Christians' learning to hear reflects the tension between revelation and faith (cf. grace and free will), which characterizes the Western Christian tradition from Augustine onwards.

Augustine declared, "Everything that we need for our life of faith and our moral life can be found in what is stated explicitly in Scripture."[6] Even a quick glance at Augustine's Christian Neoplatonism will rule out the possibility that by this assertion Augustine was prohibiting theology's use of concepts beyond Scripture. Augustine was not a scholastic Protestant like Charles Hodge, pillar of the Old Princeton Theology, who proclaimed that, "The duty of the Christian theologian is to ascertain, collect, and combine all the facts which God has revealed concerning himself and our relation to him. These facts are all in the Bible."[7] Instead, Augustine's declaration meant that Scripture provides the *rule* for theology. Scripture is the *norma normans* (the "norm-making norm" or rule-making rule) for all of the diverse *normae normatae* ("normed norms") of theology.[8]

Austin Farrer offers an intriguing reversal of Augustine's view of Scripture as the rule for theology. Farrer maintains the converse: "Theology is an indispensable rule for reading the scriptures."[9] Although Farrer is careful to observe that theology "is not the substance of the word of God,"[10] given the "shattered spectrum"[11]

---

[6]"In iis quae aperte in scripturas posita sunt, inveniuntur illa omnia quae continent fidem moresque vivendi," *De doctrina christiana*, II: 14 (J. P. Migne, *Patrologia Latina* 34, 42). The English translation is taken from Edward Schillebeeckx, *Revelation and Theology*, trans. N. D. Smith (London: Sheed and Ward, 1967).

[7]Charles Hodge, "Introduction," *Systematic Theology*, in Sydney Ahlstrom, ed., *Theology in America: The Major Voices from Puritanism to Neo-Orthodoxy* (Indianapolis IN: Bobbs-Merrill, 1967) 257-58.

[8]For further discussion of this theme and its relationship to the theology of Karl Barth, see Hans Küng, *Justification: The Doctrine of Karl Barth and a Catholic Reflection*, expanded edition (Philadelphia: Westminster, 1981), especially 111-22.

[9]Austin Farrer, *The Glass of Vision* (London: Dacre Press, 1948) 146. Farrer may perhaps here serve as a surprisingly unlikely forerunner of later advocates of a regulative understanding of doctrine such as George Lindbeck.

[10]Ibid.

of contemporary theology, one is hard-pressed to see how this theological diversity can yield an "indispensable rule." The greatest problem here is not the lack of possibilities for rules, but the problem of deciding *whose* theology will be allowed or empowered to furnish the rules. As liberation theologies unceasingly remind Eurocentric Christians, theology is not written in a vacuum, but reflects and is often controlled by the social location of the theologian.[12]

So, while I agree that a theological reading of the Scriptures is necessary for the Christian community, I think that the movement of thought must flow from Scripture to theology (doctrine) and not the reverse. Of course, this view of the direction of theological reflection does not deny in any way the theological shaping of Scripture, but rather distinguishes between what Ricoeur labels "the archaeology" and "the teleology" of the text.[13] Historical investigation of the theological shaping of Scripture in the process of its formation into a canonical text should be distinguished from the subsequent and continuing theological interpretation of the final form(s) of the text by communities of faith.

Due to the limited historical evidence, the sketchy details for a precise dating of this distinction are always open to continuing debate and significant revision.[14] Although it can only be specified in the most general historical terms, the distinction between

---

[11]See Chapter 1, especially "The Theologian's Dilemma: Disorder in the Garden," for further documentation and discussion of this issue.

[12]For an introduction to these questions see Gustavo Gutiérrez, *A Theology of Liberation*, rev. ed., trans. and ed. Caridad Inda and John Eagleson (Maryknoll NY: Orbis, 1988), especially 121 ff.

[13]Paul Ricoeur, *Freud and Philosophy: An Essay in Interpretation*, trans. Denis Savage (New Haven: Yale University Press, 1970), especially 419-551. Also, Paul Ricoeur, "A Philosophical Interpretation of Freud," trans. Willis Domingo, in *The Conflict of Interpretations: Essays in Hermeneutics*, ed. Don Ihde (Evanston IL: Northwestern University Press, 1974) 161-76, especially 173-74.

[14]See Chapter 3 for more detailed discussion of some of the critical historical problems involved. A more thorough review of the historical debate surrounding the history of canon formation and Childs' proposal may be found in my dissertation, "Canonical Hermeneutics: The Theological Basis and Implications of the Thought of Brevard S. Childs" (The Southern Baptist Theological Seminary, 1987), especially chapters 1 and 3.

Christian communities in the process of canon formation and Christian communities in the ongoing process of reflection upon the final forms of the canon of Scripture is a critical one for evangelical theology. Its significance perhaps rivals the significance of the distinction in Judaism between the period of pentateuchal formation and the generations of rabbinic reflection upon *torah*. In both cases, the direction of theological reflection changes—from the shaping of traditions into Scripture to the interpretation of given traditions as Scripture. For Christian communities canon offers the rule (provides the boundaries for) the interpretation of Scripture, which is the primary source of authority for Christian theology in the evangelical tradition.

· Scripture and Tradition: Canon and "Precritical" Interpretation ·

The stereotypical Western view of the issue of Scripture and tradition is fast becoming a historical relic. The assumption that Protestants hold to *sola Scriptura* (Scripture alone) as authority for theology, while Catholics acknowledge two sources of authority (Scripture and tradition) has proven to be an inaccurate picture of both sides of the division. Gerhard Ebeling clearly perceives the dilemma:

> As the complexity of the history of the canon comes to be increasingly recognized, both of the following attitudes become untenable: it is neither permissible to deduce directly from the New Testament writings themselves the idea and limits of the canon nor to infer the existence of an independent principle of Tradition with regard to Scripture from the process of the formation of the canon.[15]

Christian theology that relies upon the authority of Scripture needs to reframe its understanding of biblical authority in language that no longer reflects the polemical battlelines drawn

---

[15]Gerhard Ebeling, " 'Sola Scriptura' and Tradition," in *The Word of God and Tradition: Historical Studies Interpreting the Divisions of Christianity*, trans. S. H. Hooke (London: Collins, 1968) 102-47, quotation at 114.

between Protestant scholasticism and Tridentine Catholicism.[16] One time-honored strategy for approaching this task is to seek to develop through the historical study of early Christianity a less fractured understanding of the role of tradition and its relationship to Scripture.

North Atlantic theologians not only need to hear the criticisms offered of Enlightenment theological traditions by liberation theologians from the Southern hemisphere; they also need to turn East and hear the voices of Orthodox Christians. While theologians of liberation call for a recovery of the biblical "preferential option for the poor," theologians of Orthodoxy call for a recovery of the biblical emphasis upon living tradition. As Georges Florovsky maintains,

> Tradition was in the Early Church, first of all, an hermeneutical principle and method. Scripture could be rightly and fully assessed and understood only in the light and in the context of the living Apostolic Tradition, which was an integral factor of Christian existence. It was so, of course, not because Tradition could add anything to what has been manifested in Scripture, but because it provided that living context, the comprehensive perspective, in which only the true "intention" and the total design of the Holy Writ, of Divine Revelation itself, could be detected and grasped.[17]

This wholistic, hermeneutical understanding of tradition in the early church bears striking affinities to Hans-Georg Gadamer's horizonal understanding of tradition that we analyzed in the

---

[16]As historical studies of the Decree on Scripture have revealed, the later interpretation of the Council of Trent as mandating a theory of revelation with two independent sources (Scripture and tradition) is inaccurate, as the Council abandoned the *"partim . . . partim"* language originally proposed for the decree. For further discussion see Hubert Jedin, *History of the Council of Trent*, 2 vols., trans. Dom Ernest Graf (New York: Thomas Nelson, 1957, 1961), especially 2:73-92.

[17]Georges Florovsky, *Bible, Church, Tradition: An Eastern Orthodox View*, vol. 1 in the *Collected Works* (Belmont MA: Nordland, 1972) 79.

second chapter.[18] It moves away from the endless regress of Enlightenment-based preoccupation with the reconstructed psychological intentions of historical authors. Instead the interpretation of Scripture moves toward a theocentric (and hence theo-logical) understanding of the canon of Scripture as the Word of God.

As an illustration of the exegetical implications of this wholistic hermeneutical understanding of tradition, we will briefly examine a passage from Augustine's *Homilies on the Gospel of John*. Augustine was preaching on the miracle of the five loaves and two fishes in John 6:1-14. He offered this powerful description of the interweaving of the literal and the symbolic into a wholistic interpretation of this passage.

> Here then something was brought near to the senses that by it the mind should be lifted up, and exhibited to the eyes, that upon it the understanding should be exercised: that the invisible God might through visible works be admired by us, and we, being lifted up to faith and purged by faith, might desire to have vision invisibly of Him, even of whom Invisible, we by visible things had knowledge.[19]

Augustine's interwoven literal-and-symbolic approach to exegesis not only characterizes his homiletical interpretations of the New Testament, but also his exegetical appropriations of the Old Testament.[20] What holds the two Testaments together is, at least in part, a typological understanding of Scripture in terms of expectation (prophecy) and fulfillment. Through a revision of such typological understanding of exegesis—rather than through an

---

[18]See especially the section of chapter 2 entitled "Tradition and Language-Gadamer." Also, this view of tradition seems to fit well with Wittgenstein's emphasis that words have meaning only in the context of forms of life, which we discussed in the section "Forms of Life and Language Games" in chapter 2.

[19]Augustine, *Tractatio in Iohannum*, 24:1, trans. in *Homilies on the Gospel According to St. John and His First Epistle*, vol. 1, (Oxford: John Henry Parker, 1848) 373.

[20]For an analysis of Augustine's joint literal and symbolic understanding of the *sensus literalis* of Scripture, with an example from his exegesis of Genesis 1:6ff, see my article, "The *Sensus Literalis*—A Hermeneutical Key to Biblical Exegesis," *Scottish Journal of Theology*, 42 (1989): 45-65.

allegorical approach that loses hermeneutical control[21]—a post-critical interpretation of Scripture can re-establish continuity with traditional (precritical) exegesis.

Florovsky offers a helpful description of the contrast between these exegetical methods.[22]

> Patristic terminology was ... rather fluent. Still there was always a clear distinction between two methods and approaches. "Allegory" was an exegetical method indeed. An allegorist dealt primarily with the texts; he searched out the ultimate meaning of Scriptural passages, sentences and even particular words, behind and beneath "the letter." On the contrary, "typology" was not an exegesis of the texts themselves, but rather an interpretation of the events. It was an historical, and not merely a philological method. It was the inner correspondence of the events themselves in the two Testaments that had to be detected, established and brought forward.[23]

A postcritical canonical hermeneutics can re-establish continuity with pre-critical interpretation of Scripture through a rehabilitation and reformulation of typological interpretation. Historical-critical study rightly polemicized against the interpretive excesses of allegorical interpretation. Its consequent rejection of allegory as a primary modern method of Scripture study contains a warning that must be heeded. On the other hand, historical-critical polemics against a typological interpretation that maintains a historical connection between type and antitype seem misplaced.

Now, of course, the direct identification of events in Scripture with "events in history" needs postcritical modification. Contrary to the patristic exegetes, it is not "the inner correspondence of the events themselves in the Two Testaments" that typology interprets, but rather the inner correspondence between various canonical witnesses to the events. Such a language-centered modification,

---

[21]For examples and analysis of this hermeneutical loss of control in Origen, see my article, "Allegorical Flights of Fancy: The Problem of Origen's Exegesis," *The Greek Orthodox Theological Review* 32 (1987): 69-88.

[22]For discussion of the debate between Jean Daniélou and R. P. C. Hanson regarding the distinction between "typology" and "allegory," see my "Allegorical Flights of Fancy" article and references cited there.

[23]Florovsky, *Bible, Church, Tradition*, 30-31.

however, does not vitiate the logic and power of typological interpretation. For as Wittgenstein asserts, "It is in language [*Sprache*] that an expectation [*Erwartung*] and its fulfillment [*Erfüllung*] make contact."[24]

In a postcritical environment, typological interpretation needs to acknowledge explicitly that language is the vehicle through which all interpretation functions. The days are gone when some spiritual "encounter"[25] with events in Scripture could create a separate "history of salvation"[26] or a special category of revelation.[27] What Jews and Christians possess are the words in the canonical texts of Scripture that bear witness to the past, create meaning in the present, and point toward the future.

· Scripture and History:
Canon and Historical-Critical Interpretation ·

Although postcritical canonical hermeneutics seeks to re-establish continuity with the long tradition of biblical interpretation before the Enlightenment, it does not represent a rejection of historical-critical methods of biblical study in favor of some romanticized "return" to "precritical" interpretation. Canonical hermeneutics is genuinely *post*critical. This view of biblical interpretation seeks to incorporate the gains made through historical-critical study of the Bible, while moving beyond the paradigm in an effort to deal with some of its inadequacies. In this section we consider some of the liabilities of historical-critical interpretation as practiced in the

---

[24]Ludwig Wittgenstein, *Philosophische Untersuchungen/ Philosophical Investigations*, trans. G. E. M. Anscombe (Oxford: Basil Blackwell, 1963) I: 445.

[25]For a striking example, see Emil Brunner's work, *Truth as Encounter*, trans. Amandus W. Loos and David Cairns (Philadelphia: Westminster Press, 1964).

[26]See Childs' description of the decline of the Biblical Theology movement with its salvation history theme in *Biblical Theology in Crisis* (Philadelphia: Westminster Press, 1970).

[27]See Ronald Thiemann, *Revelation and Theology: The Gospel as Narrated Promise* (Notre Dame: University of Notre Dame Press, 1985) 1-46. For my discussion of Thiemann's argument, see Chapter 1, "The Formal Problem: The Crisis of Revelation-Centered Prolegomena."

twentieth century and see how a postcritical canonical hermeneutics might address some of these weaknesses.

The first and most obvious weakness of twentieth-century
historical criticism lies in its overidentification of Scripture and
history. Perhaps the clearest example of this tendency lies in the
"history of salvation" (*Heilsgeschichte*) school that was so popular
during the middle of the century. For example, John Baillie in his
classic *The Idea of Revelation in Recent Thought* offers the following
description of the relationship between the Bible and history:

> The Bible is essentially the story of the acts of God. As has often been
> pointed out, its most striking difference from *all* other religions lies in its
> *historical* character. Other sacred books are composed mainly of oracles
> which communicate what profess to be timeless truths about universal
> being or timeless prescriptions for the construct of life and worship. But
> the Bible is mainly a record of what God has done. Those parts of it
> which are not in a strict sense historiographic are nevertheless placed in
> a *definite historical frame and setting* which they presuppose at *every*
> point.[28]

In addition to Baillie's rather obvious ethnocentric over-
simplification of the historical nature of Christianity as compared
to other religions, the massive claims that he makes for the
historical character of all of the Bible are rather astounding. Lest
the reader think this is simply a rhetorical overstatement on Baillie's part rather than a tenaciously held theological claim, one only
has to examine how Baillie interprets a book of the Bible that is
"not in a strict sense historiographic." For example, Baillie extends
his historical assertion in this claim about the Psalms:

> The Book of Psalms, again, would not usually be classified as a historical
> book, yet the golden thread running through it all is God's saving action
> in leading Israel out of Egypt and into the promised land.[29]

---

[28]John Baillie, *The Idea of Revelation in Recent Thought* (London: Oxford University Press, 1956) 50, emphases added.

[29]Ibid., 51. Baillie's "golden thread" may remind evangelical Protestant readers
of the "scarlet thread" that popular piety claims to find throughout the Scripture.

The problem here is not that there are not important historical issues to be dealt with in the study of the Psalms. In fact, many of the historical issues of Psalms interpretation are notoriously vexed and difficult. For example, the overwhelming majority of psalms have been contested as to their dating—seen as pre-exilic by some scholarly commentators and postexilic by others (with the obvious exception of the "weeping by the waters of Babylon" Psalm 137!) The point is rather that the historical reconstruction of the origin of the Psalms is not going to furnish the key to their use in the life of the Christian church and their theological significance. The Psalms are clearly religious poetry, not historical prose. So, while historical study may prove to be quite valuable, to think of the Psalms in "a definite historical frame and setting that they presuppose in every point" is to make a serious category mistake.

The consequences for Christian doctrine of this overidentification of Scripture and history are serious. The spiritual life of the Scripture "withers away" amidst the endless, dry "scientific" debates over the historical reconstruction of the Bible. The Bible no longer speaks to the Christian community as the Word of God, but instead is reduced to "scientific evidence" to support the truth of the community's claims against the challenges of other groups.

Maurice Blondel pictures the situation well in his critique of the historicism of an earlier generation:

> A sort of dialectical evolutionism is deduced from this scientific determinism which claims to have penetrated the spiritual sources of the living chain of souls because it has verified the external joints of the links which are no more than its corpse.[30]

In short, the historicism resulting from an overidentification of Scripture and history is subject to serious theological critique.

In addition to this danger of historicism the contemporary critique of metaphysics raises major philosophical doubts regarding the

---

[30]Maurice Blondel, "History and Dogma," in *The Letter on Apologetics and Dogma*, trans. Alexander Dru and Illtyd Trethowan (London: Harvill Press, 1964) 240.

epistemology of the doctrine of revelation,[31] which mediates between historical events and the Christian community in the view
of these history of salvation theologians.

For example, William Temple's classic characterization of revelation asserts, "Its essence is intercourse of mind and event."[32] This
definition shows how the metaphysical and the historical aspects
of the history of salvation understanding are intertwined. The critique of metaphysics, which we briefly examined in Chapter 2,
signifies that "mind" is no longer a philosophically secure category, but perhaps a bewitching illusion (e.g., Wittgenstein).[33] The
critique of historicism contends that "event" is not a secure category either. Historical events are not objective facts, but their
reality is shaped by their perception and interpretation.[34] So, biblical theologies dependent upon this "historical" understanding of
revelation are left with both feet firmly planted in mid-air.

Even such an eminent historical-critical scholar as Raymond E.
Brown has conceded the limitations of historical-critical exegesis
for determining the relationship between Scripture and Christian
doctrine. Brown holds to a view of the primacy of "the literal
sense" of Scripture (in the narrow sense of authorial intention)[35]
over canonical levels of meaning.[36] He then makes the startling
admission,

---

[31]For further discussion of these issues in a more recent context, see Chapter
1, especially the discussion of the philosophical critique of the traditional doctrine
of revelation, in the section analyzing "The Formal Problem."

[32]William Temple, *Nature, Man, and God* (London: Macmillan, 1935) 316.

[33]See especially the section in Chapter 2 entitled "The Bewitchment of Language—Wittgenstein."

[34]For a sparkling exposition of this theme by a modern historian, see Edward
Hallett Carr, *What Is History?* (New York: Random House, 1961). For a philosophical analysis, see Paul Ricoeur, *Time and Narrative*, vol. 1.

[35]For a historical demonstration of the limitations of Brown's definition of the
literal sense, see my article, "The *Sensus Literalis*—A Hermeneutical Key to Biblical
Exegesis," *Scottish Journal of Theology* 42 (1989): 45-65.

[36]Brown claims, "Childs decries any priority given to the literal sense and
deplores the attempt to distinguish between the literal and canonical levels of
meaning pertinent to the Bible," *Biblical Exegesis and Church Doctrine* (London:
Geoffrey Chapman, 1985) 22.

I agree that the canonical meaning of Scripture is *more normative* for Christian living; but the biblical scholar must uncover the literal sense in order that the ancient dialogue which took place in the canon-forming process . . . may remain open.[37]

Brown's view here of the role of biblical scholarship seems to be remarkably similar to Ricoeur's understanding of the task of uncovering the "archaeology" of the text.[38] Given the concession that canonical meanings are "more normative for Christian living" and hence, presumably, normative for the thought and practices of the Christian community, an approach to canonical hermeneutics that emphasizes historical levels of meaning should be highly attractive.

The modified version of Childs' canonical hermeneutics, which we have been exploring in this book as the central theme of prolegomena for a postcritical evangelical theology, seeks to overcome the weaknesses of historicism. While critical history is essential for the study of Scripture, its function is an "archaeological" rather than a magisterial one. Recovering "the ancient dialogue that took place in the canon-forming process" is a necessary but subordinate process to discovering the meaning of Scripture for the life and thought of Christian communities today. As Gadamer has shown, a host of historical horizons of meaning intervenes between the time of formation of an ancient text and its contemporary appropriation as a "classic" (or, in the case of the Bible, a canonical text).[39] The hermeneutically aware interpreter must take into account these intervening levels (e.g., the history of exegesis of a biblical text), as well as his or her own horizon of meaning, as part

---

[37]Ibid., emphasis added.

[38]See the discussion of this distinction above in the first section of this chapter. Of course, Ricoeur would reject Brown's restriction of the *sensus literalis* to a historically reconstructed authorial intentionality. See Paul Ricoeur, *Essays on Biblical Interpretation*, ed. Lewis Mudge (Philadelphia: Fortress Press, 1980) and *Interpretation Theory: Discourse and the Surplus of Meaning* (Fort Worth TX: Texas Christian University Press, 1976).

[39]For a brief exposition of the role of Gadamer's hermeneutics in canonical hermeneutics, see Chapter 2, "Tradition and Language—Gadamer." See also my discussion of "The Hermeneutical Notion of Tradition" in Chapter 3. A more detailed discussion may be found in my "Canonical Hermeneutics," Chapter 4, "Contemporary Hermeneutics: Dialogue with Canonical Hermeneutics."

of the task of listening to this ancient text speak today. In effect, a broader view of history, which includes the "teleology" of the text, replaces a narrower historical-critical view, which only is concerned about the "archaeology" of the text.

This raises an important concern about hermeneutical control. If canonical hermeneutics utilizes a multi-level model of meanings grounded in the formation and use of the biblical text, what is to prevent any historical horizon of meaning that happens to coincide with the interpreter's wishes from becoming the dominant one? How does hermeneutically-shaped biblical interpretation avoid the shoals of relativistic eisegesis? The response of canonical hermeneutics is found in the claim that the final form(s) of the text, as *used* by communities of faith over the centuries—rather than some reconstructed or purged text, whether by Marcion or later exegetes —should be normative for interpretation.[40]

So, on the one hand, the value of historical-critical exegesis in illuminating the process of the development of the biblical texts to their final forms(s) and in preventing anachronistic eisegesis is essential. On the other hand, because of the inadequacies and limitations of historical-critical exegesis in determining the canonical meanings of these texts for communities that use them as Scripture, historical-critical methods should play a more circumscribed role, which allows space for critical dialogue with traditional interpretation.

In summary, canonical hermeneutics incorporates historical-critical study of the Bible into its model of biblical interpretation, but with a more modest understanding of the role of historical authority and evidence in the life and thought of the Christian community. As Patrick Sherry describes the relationship,

> In the case of Christianity I do think there is some causal and logical connection between the present responses, activities, and so on of believers, and certain historical events; any complete description and

---

[40]See Chapter 3, especially the section entitled "The Final Form of the Text," for a discussion of this claim.

understanding of Christian "forms of life" must take such connections into account.[41]

Kierkegaard was right when he saw that historical knowledge alone cannot compel faith. Rather, the Christian community points to "historical point[s] of departure" for the life of faith under the rule of Scripture.

· Scripture and Pattern: Canon and Postcritical Interpretation ·

The journey of canonical hermeneutics from traditional through historical-critical to postcritical interpretation of Scripture is a long and arduous one for evangelical Christians. This section will describe one possible path for this journey of thought. We will point out three landmarks along the way in our argument: (1) the purpose of Scripture, (2) the interplay of image and event, and (3) the pattern of the language of Scripture.

Purpose

The question of canonical hermeneutics begins with the question of the purpose of Scripture. Why do Christians read these particular books and not others? Why do evangelical Christians claim that God speaks to them through these particular books in a way that is different from all other works—whether "classic" or contemporary?

If evangelical theology is going to move beyond the Scylla of fideism and the Charybdis of relativism, the question of the purpose of Scripture must be confronted. The Scylla of fideism commonly takes the following form: "I know from personal experience (or communal affiliation) that God speaks to me through the Bible, and that settles the matter. No further thought or discussion is necessary." There is a variant form of this Scylla of fideism that sounds like historical evidentialism: "I know from the 'facts' of the

---

[41]Patrick Sherry, "Is Religion A 'Form of Life'?" *American Philosophical Quarterly*, 9 (1972): 159-67, at 167.

Bible that God has spoken to me through the Bible, and that settles the matter."[42]

The Charybdis of relativism often takes the form of existential theology among evangelical Christians. "I know from personal experience that the Bible is true *for me* (or for my community) and that's all I need to know (or all I can know). I can't say whether it is true for you."

When these common expressions of fideism and relativism among evangelical Christians are compared, the striking observation is their remarkable similarity. For all the disclaimers issued by the propositionalists, the location of both Scylla and Charybdis in the sea of personal religious experience (first charted for Protestants by Friedrich Schleiermacher) is certainly ironic.[43]

So, if the authority of Scripture for evangelical theology is not to be grounded solely and finally in religious experience (whether personal or intra-communal), then some sort of case must be made for the authority of Scripture based upon its internally and externally observable *use* by Christians. In other words, humanly observed (*coram humanibus*), the authority of the Bible rests upon the ways in which it has functioned and continues to function as Scripture within the Christian community. To describe the matter

---

[42]The Old Princeton Theology of Charles Hodge fits into this pattern, especially when it is coupled with the pietism of the tradition. The latter was expressed in such events as the Sunday afternoon prayer meetings led by Princeton Seminary professors, who taught and wrote like Protestant scholastics all week, and prayed and testified like Protestant pietists on Sunday. It was this blend of warm-hearted and "cold-headed" religion that made the evangelical Calvinism of the Old Princeton Theology so attractive to Southern Baptists in the Charleston tradition, like James P. Boyce. For Hodge's propositionalism, see his *Systematic Theology*, 3 vols. (New York: Charles Scribner's Sons, 1872).

[43]See Friedrich Schleiermacher, *Speeches on Religion to Its Cultured Despisers*, trans. John Oman (New York: Harper and Row, 1958), and *The Christian Faith*, trans. H.R. Mackintosh and J. S. Stewart, 2 vols. (New York: Harper and Row, 1963). For his hermeneutics, see Friedrich Schleiermacher, *Hermeneutics: The Handwritten Manuscripts*, trans. James Duke and Jack Forstman (Missoula: Scholars Press, 1977). Hans Frei offers a careful analysis of the "sea change" in biblical interpretation effected by Schleiermacher (*The Eclipse of Biblical Narrative: A Study in Eighteenth and Nineteenth Century Hermeneutics* [New Haven CT: Yale University Press, 1974] 282-306).

from a theocentric perspective (*coram Deo*), the authority of Scripture rests upon the purpose for which God gave the Scripture. Or, in the words of John Baillie, "The true distinction between the canonical books and the others is not in the degree of their inspiration but in the *purpose* for which [they were] given."[44]

In summary, the first step towards a postcritical canonical hermeneutic is to focus upon the purpose of Scripture, which may be ascertained through its use by Christian communities and which is observable both internally and externally.

Image and Event

The second step on our journey of thought to a postcritical canonical hermeneutics is to examine the hermeneutical interplay between image and event in the Bible as Scripture. Here we utilize the pioneering work of Austin Farrer, which seeks to connect historical events with traditional (precritical) meanings. Although Farrer's work is metaphysical, rather than postcritical, it offers a useful intermediate stage on our journey towards a postcritical hermeneutic.

In *The Glass of Vision* Farrer offers the following description of revelation as the interplay of image and event.

> The great images interpreted the events of Christ's ministry, death, and resurrection, and the events interpreted the images; the interplay of the two is revelation. Certainly the events without the images would be no revelation at all, and the images without the events would remain shadows on the clouds. The events by themselves are not revelation, for they do not by themselves reveal the divine work which is accomplished in them.[45]

This dialectical interaction moves a major step away from historicist approaches to revelation, while avoiding the historical relativism typically associated with philosophical hermeneutics in the idealist tradition. Farrer understands revelation as neither just "the historical facts," nor simply an individual or group's

---

[44]Baillie, *The Idea of Revelation*, 118, emphasis added.
[45]Farrer, *The Glass of Vision*, 43.

understanding of the truth. Instead, there is a hermeneutical dialectic that incorporates greater recognition of the intertextuality of Scripture.[46] The Bible is seen as a "work," rather than simply as a diverse collection or conglomeration of traditions of Jewish and Christian origins.[47]

Such an intertextual emphasis has important consequences for biblical interpretation in two different directions. First, it provides a connection with traditional (precritical) biblical hermeneutics, which simply assumed the unity of Scripture as a hermeneutical axiom. For example, non-Marcionite biblical interpretation in the early church—whether typological or allegorical, whether "Alexandrian" or "Antiochene"—interpreted the Scripture intertextually as God's authoritative story for the church. Even when it saw textual differences and discrepancies, these were characteristically attributed to the providence of God. Perhaps the most dramatic example of this axiom is Origen's doctrine of "heavenly deception."[48]

The second direction of the move toward intertextuality is modern literary critical hermeneutics. In previous chapters we have already examined Paul Ricoeur's dialectical theory of reading[49] and hermeneutics of testimony[50] for their value in clarifying

---

[46]Although some parallels between Farrer's hermeneutical interplay and Schleiermacher's famous hermeneutical circle are clearly present, the different elements (Schleiermacher, text and reader; Farrer, image and event) should also be noted. For further discussion of the hermeneutical circle from the perspective of Gadamer's hermeneutics, see David Couzens Hoy, *The Critical Circle: Literature, History, and Philosophical Hermeneutics* (Berkeley: University of California Press, 1978). For an intriguing modification of the hermeneutical circle from the perspective of evangelical New Testament scholarship, see Grant Osborne, *The Hermeneutical Spiral: A Comprehensive Introduction to Biblical Interpretation* (Downers Grove IL: InterVarsity Press, 1991).

[47]For a similar view stressing biblical imagery from a literary critical perspective, see Northrop Frye, *The Great Code: The Bible and Literature* (New York: Harcourt, Brace, and Jovanovich, 1982).

[48]For a detailed exegetical analysis of Origen's hermeneutics, including his doctrine of divine deception, see Karen Jo Torjesen, *Hermeneutical Procedure and Theological Method in Origen's Exegesis* (Berlin: Walter de Gruyter, 1986).

[49]See Chapter 2, "Reading and Levels of Meaning-Ricoeur."

[50]See Chapter 3, "The Incorporation of Sociological and Literary Approaches."

and modifying Childs' canonical approach to biblical interpretation. Farrer's dialectic of image and event foreshadows the
key role that intertextuality is to play in new literary approaches
to biblical interpretation[51] and the New Yale Theology.[52] Thus, the
move towards intertextuality, through a dialectic of image and
event, both begins the process of re-establishing hermeneutical
continuity with traditional (precritical) exegesis and foreshadows
the new postcritical literary hermeneutics.

Although Farrer's hermeneutical interplay between image and
event provides a major step away from the limitations of the
historicist approaches, it only represents an intermediate step in
the process of developing a postcritical canonical hermeneutics.
Careful examination of Farrer's method reveals that, while it is
able to respond to the critique of historicism, it fails to respond to
the critique of metaphysics. Indeed the great weakness of Farrer's
approach lies in its positivistic metaphysical supernaturalism. For
example, Farrer asserts that,

> The choice, use and combination of images made by Christ and the
> Spirit must be simply a supernatural work: otherwise Christianity is an
> illusion.[53]

Such a rigid view of the images of Scripture seems to transfer
many of the difficulties with a literalist hermeneutic of the words
of Scripture into a rigid hermeneutic of the images (or associated
doctrines) of Scripture. Where is the freedom of the Spirit in such
a view? Why does such a view ignore the Puritan conviction that

---

[51]John Barton has made the claim that Childs' canonical approach should be
understood as a form of structuralism and is "formally parallel" to the New Criticism movement in literature (*Reading the Old Testament* [London: Darton,
Longman, and Todd, 1984] 133).

[52]See Brett, *Biblical Criticism,"* 156ff, and Mark I. Wallace, *The Second Naiveté:
Barth, Ricoeur, and the New Yale Theology,* Studies in American Biblical Hermeneutics (Macon GA: Mercer University Press, 1990), especially 89ff.

[53]Farrer, *The Glass of Vision,* 109.

"God hath yet more light to be revealed in his Holy Word"[54]? The hermeneutical interplay of image and event fails to account for the multiple levels of meaning that Christians discover in the Bible as Scripture. In short, Farrer's approach leaves us with a dogmatic metaphysics rather than a dogmatic view of biblical inspiration. Therefore, another step needs to be taken in order arrive at a postcritical hermeneutics that takes into account both the critique of historicism and the critique of metaphysics.

Pattern

The final landmark on our journey of thought toward a postcritical canonical hermeneutics is the development of a theological understanding of pattern in Scripture. In the second chapter we described some postcritical categories derived from the later Wittgenstein's thought that help to illumine canonical hermeneutics.[55] Beginning with an understanding of meaning as use, we sought to describe *functionally* the canon of Scripture as the norm for language games rooted in the practices of Christian forms of life. For evangelical Christians in a postcritical era the authority of Scripture lies in its use, rather than in some foundationalist theory of its inspiration.

This approach raises the question of what Christians discover in Scripture, as they use it to guide and warrant their practices, both individually and communally. Wittgenstein's analysis of "the dawning of an aspect" points toward the role of pattern in all perception and knowledge.[56] As Garrett Green explains:

> Everything we perceive or know depends on our grasping a particular *pattern* by which diverse parts present themselves as a whole. We do not construct the whole piecemeal by assembling discrete elements into organized wholes; rather, having a world *means* seeing according to a

---

[54]This quotation has been attributed to the Puritan Separatist John Robinson. Timothy George has offered a thorough historical assessment of Robinson's theology and ecclesiology in *John Robinson and the English Separatist Tradition* (Macon GA: Mercer University Press, 1982).

[55]See the section, "The Formulation of Postcritical Categories," in Chapter 2.

[56]Wittgenstein, *PI*, II: 193ff.

pattern, having a vision of how things hang together as the precondition for recognizing the parts *as* parts in the first place.[57]

For canonical hermeneutics the patterns that Christians discover in Scripture are the elements they use to guide and warrant their individual and communal religious practices. So, for a postcritical evangelical theology, a Christian practice is "biblical" if it conforms to the patterns of Scripture rather than if it can be warranted by an appropriate prooftext.

This understanding of biblical warrant is quite important for the development of Christian doctrine. To take a famous example, the Nicene Trinitarianism of Athanasius is not "more biblical" because Athanasius was able to cite more or better biblical prooftexts to support his view than was Arius. In fact, historical study reveals that probably the reverse was the case. Arius had the better prooftexts![58] Athanasius represents biblical orthodoxy because the doctrine of God that he advocated conforms more closely to the *pattern* of the saving God made known in Jesus Christ through Holy Scripture.

In order to elucidate further the significance of pattern for a postcritical canonical hermeneutics, we examine two examples from Wittgenstein that clarify and extend themes from Childs' exegesis in the context of the Christian canon.

The first example is Wittgenstein's discussion of the problem of confusing the meaning of a name with the bearer of a name. Wittgenstein asserts:

> It is important to note that the word "meaning" is being used illicitly if it is used to signify the thing that "corresponds" to the word. That is to

---

[57]Garrett Green, "The Bible As . . .: Fictional Narrative and Scriptural Truth," in *Scriptural Authority and Narrative Interpretation*, ed. Garrett Green (Philadelphia: Fortress Press, 1987) 79-96, at 85. For further discussion of this theme cf. William Placher, *Unapologetic Theology: A Christian Voice in a Pluralistic Conversation* (Louisville KY: Westminster/John Knox, 1989) 123-37.

[58]Arthur McGill offers a provocative theological accounting of the significance of the debate between Arius and Athanasius in *Suffering: A Test of Theological Method* (Philadelphia: Westminster Press 1968)," 64-82. Maurice Wiles has provided a number of controversial historical studies in this area, especially his spirited "In Defense of Arius," *Journal of Theological Studies* 13 (1962): 339-47.

confuse the meaning of the name with the *bearer* of the name. When Mr.
N. N. dies one says that the bearer of the name dies, not that the
meaning dies. And it would be nonsensical to say that, for if the name
ceased to have meaning it would make no sense to say "Mr. N. N. is
dead."[59]

Wittgenstein demonstrates the conceptual error of limiting the
meaning of a name to the historical life of its bearer. Thus we must
look to the pattern of use of a name to understand the full range
of its meanings.[60] This distinction clarifies Childs' use of the terms
"canonical" and "historical" for various biblical figures. The historical Amos preaches only gloom and doom; the canonical Amos
preaches God's judgment and mercy.[61] The canonical Paul is
clearly identified with the book of Ephesians, whether the historical Paul wrote it or not.[62] The interpretation of a biblical figure
is not restricted to the (often uncertain) historically reconstructed
limits of his or her life.

The second example pushes this distinction even further, as
Wittgenstein argues for the utility of "blurred concepts."

One might say that the concept "game" is a concept with blurred
edges.—"But is a blurred concept a concept at all?"—Is an indistinct
photograph a picture of a person at all? Is it even always an advantage
to replace an indistinct picture by a sharp one? Isn't the indistinct one
often exactly what we need?[63]

Childs has shown that a blurred concept seems to be exactly
what the redactors of biblical books have left for us. The parade
example here is the book of Isaiah, especially chapters 40ff. Childs
argues that,

---

[59]Wittgenstein, *PI*, I: 40. For a related discussion see Ludwig Wittgenstein,
Philosophical Grammar, trans. A. J. Kenny (Berkeley: University of California Press,
1974) 64.

[60]James Barr argues for a similar conclusion on philological grounds in *The
Semantics of Biblical Language* (Oxford: Oxford University Press, 1961).

[61]See the discussion of Amos in Chapter 1, in the section "The Material Problem: The Decline of the Historical-Critical Paradigm."

[62]See the exegetical example of Ephesians in Chapter 3.

[63]Wittgenstein, *PI*, I: 71.

> Even though the message was once addressed to real people in a particular historical situation—whether according to the model of Begrich or Muilenburg is indecisive—the canonical editors of this tradition employed the material in such a way as to eliminate almost entirely those concrete features and to subordinate the original message to a new role within the canon.[64]

Childs then interprets the blurring as important for the theological meaning of the entire book.

> First Isaiah spoke mainly of judgment to pre-exilic Israel. Conversely Second Isaiah's message was predominantly one of forgiveness. But in their canonical context these historical distinctions have been frequently blurred in order to testify to a theology which was directed to subsequent generations of Israelites.[65]

Besides exegetical examples that relate to the role of blurring in the canonical shaping of an entire biblical book, the notion of a blurred concept can have great utility at lower levels as well. For instance, consider the redactional shaping of the Hebrew word *'adam* in the early narratives of Genesis. At times the word seems definitely to refer to humanity or the human (e.g., Gen 1:26, cf. 2:5,7), while at other times it seems to serve as a specific proper name—"Adam" (e.g., Gen 4:25). Much of the futile polemics that have surrounded these passages in evangelical Protestant circles could be eliminated if we could acknowledge that the rabbis left us, intentionally or not, with blurred concepts. In other words, the theological meaning of the creation narratives of Genesis does not hinge upon debates over their historicity.

The idea of the utility of a blurred concept has another important application for canonical hermeneutics. This relates to the boundaries of the canon itself. In the discussion of the deuterocanonical books in Chapter 3, I argued for a more flexible view regarding the exact boundaries of the canon that acknowledged the

---

[64]Brevard Childs, *Introduction to the Old Testament as Scripture* (Philadelphia: Fortress Press, 1979) 325.
[65]Childs, *IOTS*, 327.

diverse claims of Christian traditions.[66] Given a functional notion of the formation of the canon—viz., as Christian communities used these books, they discovered the Word of God in them—it should be possible to grant that historically different groups of Christians have heard the Word of God or not heard the Word of God in different books on the periphery of the canon. In other words, the canon has a "firm core" and a rather "blurred circumference."[67] In short, canon is an "indistinct concept." As Wittgenstein reminds us, "Isn't the indistinct one often exactly what we need?"

Now that we have completed our three-stage journey towards a postcritical canonical hermeneutics, the next step is to look ahead and begin to envision a canonical model of exposition for Christian doctrine. As we begin this exploration of the language of Christian doctrine in the final chapter, Hans Frei offers some valuable insight:

> Christian theology must in the first place pay heed to the language of the Christian community from the Bible to modernity, understood as an organic *pattern* possessing its own integrity, its own complex logic and highly varying relations to other forms of language and life.[68]

In this view, Christian doctrine becomes primarily an exercise in redescribing the concepts of faith, rather than an attempt at developing apologetic arguments to explain and defend the faith to those outside the Christian community.[69] Given this more modest perspective on the nature and function of Christian theology, we will now investigate some preliminary application of canonical hermeneutics to the doctrine of God.

---

[66]See the discussion in Chapter 3 at the beginning of the section entitled "Criticisms and Modifications."

[67]I am indebted to John Barton for some of this imagery, even though he is certainly not an advocate of canonical hermeneutics. See especially his *People of the Book? The Authority of the Bible in Christianity* (London: S.P.C.K., 1988).

[68]Hans W. Frei, "An Afterword: Eberhard Busch's Biography of Karl Barth," in *Karl Barth in Re-View: Posthumous Works Reviewed and Assessed*, ed. H.-Martin Rumscheidt (Pittsburgh PA: Pickwick Press, 1981) 95-116, at 104.

[69]Ibid., 110-11.

CONCLUSION: TOWARDS
A CANONICAL MODEL OF
THE DOCTRINE OF GOD

The aim of this final chapter is frankly speculative in that it seeks
to explore some ways in which a postcritical evangelical theology
shaped by canonical hermeneutics might move from biblical
interpretation to doctrinal exposition.

This effort is a preliminary one. No claim is made for any
comprehensiveness—whether biblical, historical or conceptual—
regarding the many diverse traditions of Christian thought about
God. Rather, I am attempting to organize constructively and reflect
hermeneutically upon some "fragments" of thought in the service
of the further articulation by Christian communities of their
experience with the *magnum mysterium* of the Triune God.[1]

The approach will be restricted to the development of the
doctrine of the Trinity, rather than considering the variety of ways
in which Christian theologians have discussed the doctrine of the
one God. The principal reason for this limitation is that I am
convinced by Karl Rahner's arguments that it was a mistake for
systematic theology (beginning in the medieval scholastic era)[2] to
divorce the theological treatises on the one God and the Trinity.[3]
The God whom Christians claim to know is specifically God the
Father of our Lord Jesus Christ, who is revealed in our hearts
through the witness of the Holy Spirit.

---

[1]My indebtedness to the brilliant though eccentric philosophical theology of
Søren Kierkegaard is evidenced throughout this chapter. See especially Søren
Kierkegaard, *Philosophical Fragments or A Fragment of Philosophy*, 2d ed., trans.
David F. Swenson and Howard V. Hong (Princeton: Princeton University Press,
1962). I am especially indebted to Gene Outka and Paul Holmer for initial intro-
ductions to the thought of Kierkegaard.

[2]Such a separation has continued to characterize most of Protestant theology
as well. For a notable recent exception see Frederick Herzog's *God-Walk: Liberation
Shaping Dogmatics* (Maryknoll NY: Orbis, 1988).

[3]Karl Rahner, *The Trinity*, trans. Joseph Donceel (New York: Herder and
Herder, 1970).

Despite all these delimitations, I realize that the audacity of attempting even such a modestly-defined constructive theological task in our deconstructed, postmodern world is considerable. Nevertheless, there is comfort in the recollection that even "crumbs"[4] of thought may occasionally prove to be more reliable pointers to Christian truth than the most elaborated systems of idealistic philosophy.[5] For, as Kierkegaard saw, the great danger of construing the Christian faith through idealistic philosophy is that one will build marvelous "palaces of thought" in the sky that are irrelevant to the "humble earthly shacks" where the people of God daily dwell and seek to live the truth.

Beginning with the Hellenistic Platonism of Justin Martyr and Origen, Christian philosophical thinkers have been perennially tempted, through an "enchantment" with abstract being, to deviate from the quest to love the God of the Bible with all of their minds. This enchantment, which we described in chapter 2 as "the bewitchment of being,"[6] is nowhere more apparent than in philosophical treatments of the doctrine of God, both ancient and modern.[7]

---

[4]The literal translation of the Danish *"Smuler"* in Kierkegaard's *Philosophical Fragments* is "crumbs."

[5]I would contend that such is the case with Kierkegaard's "crumbs" in contrast to "the system" of Hegel. For Kierkegaard's refutation of Hegelianism, in addition to *Philosophical Fragments*, see the ironically titled *Concluding Unscientific Postscript*, trans. David F. Swenson and Walter Lowrie (Princeton: Princeton University Press, 1941).

[6]See the section of Chapter 2 entitled "The Bewitchment of Being—Kierkegaard" for further discussion of this issue.

[7]Historically, ontological speculation on the doctrine of the Trinity has often been kept within bounds by a theologian's adherence to the *regula fidei*. Two outstanding ancient examples are Origen's tendencies towards Gnosticism (cf. particularly his *Commentary on John*, XIII: 58-60; XX: 20 [*Die Grieschen Christlichen Schriftsteller der Ersten Drei Jahrhunderte: Origenes Werke* (Leipzig: J. C. Hinrichs, 1899-1976), vol. 4, 288-91, 352]) and Augustine's Neoplatonic speculations (*De Trinitate*, Books VIII and X, trans. Stephen McKenna, *The Trinity*, The Fathers of the Church: A New Translation, vol. 45 [Washington, DC: Catholic University of America Press, 1963], 243-67, 291-313). A medieval example of the scholastic extension of Augustine's *vestigia trinitatis* may be found in Bonaventure's *De triplici via* (*On the Threefold Way*). As a modern example, Paul Tillich's theology

In the following "fragments," I have sought, on the one hand, to avoid the perils of ontological preoccupation, particularly those of the "Hegelian vortex" variety.[8] On the other hand, I have attempted to distance this approach to the Trinity from an eighteenth- and nineteenth-century Protestant view of doctrine as a collection and systematization of "facts."[9] Modern analytical philosophy has seriously challenged the idea of historical "facts," claiming that the notion is systematically ambiguous, and thus of little utility for the definition and grounding of Christian doctrine.[10]

The leading theme of the reflections in this chapter—their *leitmotiv*—is the description of the Trinity as "bounded Mystery." This paradoxical view of the Trinity is dependent upon a regulative notion of Christian doctrine, which understands doctrine based upon what it does, its function. From this perspective, doctrine provides "negative guidelines" that bound the mysteries of faith.[11] I am attempting to show that the understanding of the Trinity as bounded Mystery discovers truth in the tension of paradox.

Before the theme of the Trinity as bounded Mystery can be examined and discussed, the chapter must first consider some of the problems raised in this transition from a canonical view of Scripture to the doctrine of God. The first and most obvious

---

offers a classic illustration of this problem. See his doctrine of God: "Being and God," *Systematic Theology* (Chicago: University of Chicago Press, 1951), 1:163-289, especially 163-203. In the case of Karl Rahner, his ontological enchantment is moderated by his self-restriction within the boundaries of "official trinitarian doctrine" (Rahner, *The Trinity*, especially contrasting 49-79 with 82-99).

[8]Cf. especially the central Hegelian notion of *Aufhebung*, which creates the dynamic of this dialectical whirlwind.

[9]See, for example, the work of Charles Hodge, discussed in Chapter 4 (*Systematic Theology*, 3 vols. [New York: Charles Scribner's Sons, 1872], 1:1-17).

[10]For further discussion, see the section of Chapter 2 entitled, "Tradition and Language—Gadamer."

[11]I am, of course, indebted to George Lindbeck for this regulative view of doctrine (*The Nature of Doctrine: Religion and Theology in a Postliberal Age* [Philadelphia: Westminster Press, 1984]). As will become apparent later in this chapter, although I have adopted much of Lindbeck's functional view of the nature of doctrine, I differ from him rather sharply on the nature of Scripture.

problem is that of biblical warrants for the doctrine of the Trinity. Next, the linguistic problems of classical Western trinitarian terminology are briefly considered. Then the critical matter of the nature and function of Christian doctrine is cursorily examined in general terms, with the aim of further explicating the modified regulative view to be applied to the Trinity in the remainder of this chapter.

Following these prolegomena, it will be possible to discuss the Trinity as bounded Mystery. In order to support the argument that this view of the Trinity enables the discovery of truth (*coram humanibus*) in the tension of paradox, three fundamental tensions in the doctrine of God will be explored. The first tension—unity and multiplicity—includes the classical tension between modalism and tritheism, as well as the modern tension between the psychological and social. In examining the second fundamental tension— the eschatological tension between "already" and "not yet"—the differing understandings of God found in propositional revelation, process theology, and eschatological theology are briefly examined. The third fundamental tension—God's power and God's goodness —reflects upon the contemporary theological question of God's relation to suffering. The chapter concludes with a brief hermeneutical epilogue that transposes "canon" from Scripture to musical praise, as Christians "sing the doctrine of the Trinity."

· The Christian Doctrine of God as Trinity ·

Theological reflection concerning a contemporary doctrine of the Trinity must take account of the long and complex history of Christian thought on this subject.[12] A hermeneutical exposition of the doctrine of the Trinity should be developed through dialogue

---

[12]For a comprehensive though partisan account of the doctrine of the Trinity from a traditional Roman Catholic perspective, see Bertrand de Margerie, *The Christian Trinity in History*, trans. Edmund J. Fortman (Still River MA: St. Bede's, 1982). For more concise introductions to the early history and development of the doctrine see Bernhard Lohse, *A Short History of Christian Doctrine*, trans. F. Ernest Stoeffler (Philadelphia: Fortress Press, 1966) 37-70; and J. N. D. Kelly, *Early Christian Doctrines*, 2d ed. (New York: Harper and Row, 1960) 83-137, 252-79.

in continuity with this tradition.[13] Not surprisingly, our canonical approach to this area begins with a consideration of the question of biblical warrants for the doctrine of the Trinity.

Biblical Warrants

It is obvious that the Bible does not present a fully-developed idea of God as Trinity. Rather the Scriptures allow enough plurality and pluriformity within the non-monadic Oneness of God to permit the later development of explicit trinitarian notions.[14] Furthermore, particularly in the New Testament, the repeated appearance of functionally dyadic and triadic formulations referring to God offers more specific conceptual preparation for later trinitarian formulation.[15]

The major question with the biblical material in relation to the doctrine of the Trinity is not whether the Bible would *permit* such doctrinal development, but rather to what extent the language of

---

[13]Jaroslav Pelikan offers an articulate and learned defense of the importance of the principle of continuity in *Development of Christian Doctrine, Some Historical Prolegomena* (New Haven CT: Yale University Press, 1969). Pelikan uses the principle of continuity in development of doctrine as a touchstone for his magisterial history of doctrine, *The Christian Tradition*, 5 vols. (Chicago: University of Chicago Press, 1971, 1974, 1978, 1984, and 1989.).

[14]See de Margerie, *Trinity*, 3-56, for discussion and a detailed listing of biblical passages. Although de Margerie tends to err in the direction of finding too much of the later doctrine of the Trinity explicitly in the New Testament, the biblical evidence he cites clearly supports a plurality within the Oneness of God.

[15]I am especially indebted to a lecture by William L. Hendricks, entitled "Revelatory Implicates of the Threefoldness of God" (The Southern Baptist Theological Seminary, September 4, 1985), for an understanding of the functionally triadic characterization of God within the New Testament material. Hendricks particularly points to the following passages as triadic (pre-trinitarian) in character: Matt 28:19-20; Luke 3:22, 10:21-22; John 3:34-35; Rom 5:5-6; 2 Cor 13:14 (and parallels); 1 John 5:7 (cf. Old Syriac); Jude 20-21; and Rev 16:5 (cf. development through 1:8 and 4:8). Examples of dyadic forms include: John 1:1; 1 Cor 6:19, 8:6; 2 Cor 3:16-17. Also, see Jane Schaberg, *The Father, the Son, and the Holy Spirit: The Triadic Phrase in Matthew 28:19b* (Chico CA: Scholars Press, 1982), especially 1-86, 286-91, and 319-49. For the use of triads in the Ante-Nicene Fathers see Kelly, *Doctrines*, 83-108.

the New Testament authorizes trinitarian development.[16] Claims for such authorization may be made in "strong" fashion (viz., the language of the New Testament *necessitates* the subsequent development of trinitarian language) or in "weaker" fashion (viz., the language of the New Testament *warrants* the subsequent development of trinitarian language).[17]

The argument that the language of the New Testament *necessitates* the development of trinitarian language seems finally only sustainable in a circular manner. If one argues that the development is necessitated, one is forced to "discover" that trinitarian language is already implicit in the language of the New Testament. For example, Bertrand de Margerie claims that, "Jesus names the divine Third One holy Breath in order to make known the nature of his invisible procession," and further asserts that the New Testament writers were "proclaiming the mystery of the Three."[18]

Rejecting this strong form of the argument still leaves the question open as to whether trinitarian language is *warranted* or only permitted by the language of the New Testament. I would tentatively argue for the former alternative ("warranted"), based upon the following rationale. First, as previously mentioned, the triadic formulations of language about God in the New Testament

---

[16]Although the question of whether the language of the Bible about God would even allow trinitarian development is still a live one for Jewish-Christian dialogue and an occasional anti-trinitarian "Protestant," in general the historical development of the doctrine *de facto* renders the matter a *fait accompli*. If one were to pursue the anti-trinitarian position further on exegetical grounds, the results at best would be highly dubious and furthermore would favor the historical advocacy of an anachronistic "fall of the church" view (cf. Harnack).

[17]The term "warrant" is used here in the sense of "to serve as or give ground or reason for: justify" (*Webster's Seventh New Collegiate Dictionary, ad loc.*) Stephen Toulmin has offered a masterful analysis of the ways in which arguments work in his *The Uses of Argument* (Cambridge: Cambridge University Press, 1958). Toulmin further distinguishes between the offering of evidence as "warrant" and the even more indirect logical connection of the offering of evidence as "backing" for a warrant. David Kelsey utilizes Toulmin's categories to offer a descriptive analysis of the various ways theologians use Scripture to authorize theological proposals in *The Uses of Scripture in Recent Theology* (Philadephia: Fortress Press, 1975).

[18]See de Margerie, *Trinity*, 24 and 49.

offer specific conceptual preparation for later trinitarian language.[19] In these formulations God is at least rudimentarily conceived as threeness-in-oneness, rather than as plurality in general. Perhaps the musical triad offers a fitting image for this stage of development—one chord of three notes. Moreover, the triads of New Testament language both are rooted in and shape the economy of salvation, as experienced and articulated by Christian communities. This "cultural-linguistic" description of God's salvation in triadic form constitutes biblical warrant for the later development of the economic Trinity.[20] Now, as Rahner has demonstrated, given the Oneness of God, the economic Trinity and the immanent Trinity are identical axiomatically.[21] Therefore, the use of trinitarian language to refer to God-in-Godself seems warranted by the triadic language of the New Testament.

The Linguistic Shift

The classical formulations of the doctrine of the Trinity (Greek: three *hypostases* in one *ousia*; Latin: three *personae* in one *substantia*) are cast in the ancient philosophical language of Platonic universalism. Thus, for the great majority of writers in the early church what is "real" is the universal concept (cf. Plato's "forms"), rather than the concrete particular manifestations.[22] This raises major problems for persons in the post-Enlightenment West. As heirs to nominalist philosophical assumptions, we perceive the concrete individual as "real" and the universal as an abstract concept.

So, it requires a major shift of thinking for persons in this age to be able to understand how the ancient formulations could

---

[19]I am not here arguing that this preparation is in any way intentional on the part of the New Testament writers. Rather, I am observing that the forms of this triadic language are taken up, altered, and elaborated by later writers.

[20]This cultural-linguistic approach is Lindbeck's category. See especially, *Doctrine*, 32-41. Lindbeck contends that there is a dialectical relationship between "the objectivities of religion" and religious experience.

[21]Rahner, *Trinity*, especially 21-24.

[22]Of course, this Platonic universalism is later modified in the Aristotelian limited universalism of Thomas, where the universals are in the particulars (*universalia in rebus*).

emphasize three distinct "persons" or *hypostases* without meaning three distinct centers of subjectivity or three personalities, and thereby falling into tritheism. Because of this difficulty modern theologians have sought either to replace (Barth) or to "explain" (Rahner) the concept of "person" in twentieth-century theology. Barth suggests the terminology "modes of existence,"[23] while Rahner chooses "distinct manners of subsisting."[24] In both cases, in an effort to avoid the "Scylla" of tritheism, which they view as the great modern peril of the doctrine, these formulations slide toward the "Charybdis" of modalism.[25]

Given these two options, the more conservative position of Rahner seems to be preferable to that of Barth, though not for the reasons that Rahner advocates. Rahner wants formally to retain the concept "person," while explaining it, primarily because he is required by the magisterium to accept the concept. The term "person" is part of the official trinitarian doctrine of the Catholic Church, which as a Catholic theologian he is committed to uphold. As he candidly confesses,

> It is evident that the regulation of language, which is necessary in a Church as a community of shared social worship and confession, cannot be undertaken by the single theologian at will. The only thing he can do at present is *also* to use the concept of person in the doctrine of the Trinity, and to defend it, to the extent of his power, from misunderstanding that it is threatened by. The magisterium forbids him to suppress such concepts on his own authority, but also obliges him to work on their fuller explanation.[26]

Such submission to the church's dogmatic authority as the primary ground for the retention of "person" obviously has little or no appeal or practical relevance to a Protestant theologian in the free church tradition. So, instead I will appeal to two very different reasons for the retention of the term "person."

---

[23]Karl Barth, *Church Dogmatics*, I: 1, *The Doctrine of the Word of God*, trans. G. T. Thomson (Edinburgh: T. and T. Clark, 1936), paragraph 9, "God's Three-in Oneness," 400-41, especially 408-23.

[24]Rahner, *Trinity*, 73-75, 103-15, esp. 109-15.

[25]See the discussion below on "Unity and Multiplicity."

[26]Rahner, *Trinity*, 108-109.

First, there is the aesthetic[27] reason of the place and significance of the term in the history and tradition of Christian worship.[28] One can barely conceive of the possibility of singing , "Holy, holy, holy . . . God in three modes of existence, blessed Trinity!" Even if some euphonious substitute could be devised, the proposed terminology (whether Barth's "modes of existence" or Rahner's "distinct manners of subsisting") would only increase the perceived *abstraction* and impersonality of God. The conceptual difficulty of formulating and expounding the doctrine of the Trinity only magnifies this problem. Furthermore the problem is especially vexing in this case, since such perceived abstraction is at the root of the nominalist tendency towards tritheism, which in turn motivated the attempted substitution for and explanation of "person."

A second reason for the retention of the term "person" in a contemporary doctrine of the Trinity is that fortuitously—or perhaps providentially—it is a traditional term that is able to withstand the linguistic critique of feminist theology. Only rarely does one find classical language about God, especially of a personalist nature, which is not seen by contemporary feminist scholars as tainted by patriarchy.

The term "person" is not gender-specific, even though concrete individual persons are named with gender identification. Thus, those who advocate a feminist critique of Christian language about God can perhaps discover the wisdom of *not* treating the "three persons" of the Trinity as independent centers of subjectivity, and thus avoiding a fall into gender-specific tritheism.[29] Feminist

---

[27]"Aesthetic" is used here in a classical, philosophical sense as related to the beautiful (cf. Aristotle) and not in a whimsical, so-called "artistic" sense as a mere matter of cultivated preference.

[28]On the theological legitimacy of using the *lex orandi* to shape the *lex credendi* and vice versa, see Geoffrey Wainwright, *Doxology: The Praise of God in Worship, Doctrine, and Life: A Systematic Theology* (New York: Oxford University Press, 1980), especially 218-83.

[29]Of course, one must still respond to the feminist critique that the names of each of the persons—or at least of the Father and the Son—are sexist. This objection, however, loses much of its force when one recognizes that the "persons" of the Trinity are not concrete "personalities" (i.e., individual centers of subjectivity), but rather are beyond personality and hence beyond gender.

theology points to the need to re-examine current atomistic under-standings of personhood. A feminist critique of language may then be used as a cultural force to counteract the drift toward tritheism that has accompanied the modern retention of "person" in the doctrine of the Trinity.

The Language of Doctrine

In addition to the question of biblical warrants for the doctrine of the Trinity and the linguistic problems of classical trinitarian termi-nology, there remains another major issue that we must consider before any discussion of the content of the doctrine itself: the cru-cial and complex issue of the nature and function of Christian doctrine.

George Lindbeck, in *The Nature of Doctrine*, offers a typology of models for conceptualizing religion generally and doctrine specif-ically.[30] The first type is "cognitive-propositional," which sees doctrines as providing information and making truth claims about "objective realities."[31] The second type is "experiential-expressive," which, following Protestant liberalism, views doctrines as symbol-ical of inner feelings and experience. The third type, which Lindbeck advocates, is a "cultural-linguistic" approach. In this view doctrines are understood as "instantiations of rules" that are authoritative for religious communities. As historical precedent Lindbeck points to the "rule" character of the ancient *regula fidei*.

Lindbeck dismisses the "experiential-expressive" models as es-sentially reductionistic, despite their popularity among educated circles in modern Western culture. As he contends,

> Symbolic theories, while perhaps currently the most popular, . . . tend to exclude *a priori* the traditional characteristics of doctrine. The affir-mation of the resurrection, for example, cannot easily be an enduring communal norm of belief and practice if it is seen primarily as a symbol

---

[30]Lindbeck, *Doctrine*, especially 7-12, 15-45.

[31]Lindbeck also describes a "modified cognitive-propositional" model to ac-commodate the intermediate position of modern Roman Catholic thinkers like Rahner and Lonergan, who incorporate a regulative view of doctrine into their metaphysical understandings (*Doctrine*, 104-105).

of a certain type of experience (such as that of the spiritual presence of Christ as the New Being [Tillich]) that can in principle be expressed or evoked in other ways.[32]

In addition to Lindbeck's argument for the rejection of experiential-expressive models of doctrine, Karl Barth, in his discussion of "The Word of God and Experience," has vividly traced the "primrose path" that leads from Schleiermacher to Feuerbach.[33]

When Lindbeck deals with the cognitive-propositional type of models, the possibility of refutation becomes much more difficult. Since the days of Justin Martyr, metaphysical propositions have been the classical approach for understanding the nature and function of doctrine. Perhaps one of the most significant—and certainly one of the most controversial—recent non-Catholic proposals concerning the nature of doctrine is that of Maurice Wiles. Wiles utilizes propositional assumptions about the nature of doctrine in his "revisionist" proposals for "the remaking of Christian doctrine."[34]

In his attack on Barth's rejection of "experience of the world" as the "appropriate starting point for theology," Wiles declares,

> There is no question about the religious impressiveness of this [Barth's] conception . . . But conceptions, however impressive, have to be *tested against the facts*. It seems unmistakably clear to me that we simply do not have the kind of explicit self-revelation that such a scheme requires. . . . Perhaps theology must after all abandon its claim to speak about the transcendent God; not in the paradoxical sense of becoming an atheistic theology, but in the sense that it will only speak of the effects of God as experienced, and make no attempt to speak of God in himself.[35]

In relation to the doctrine of the Trinity, Wiles' revisionist approach leads to two conclusions. First, Wiles rightly rejects what Lindbeck would call the "experiential-expressive" view that the Fathers developed the doctrine of the Trinity "because they found

---

[32]Lindbeck, *Doctrine*, 79-80.
[33]Barth, *Church Dogmatics*. I: i, paragraph 6, section 3, 226-60.
[34]Maurice Wiles, *The Remaking of Christian Doctrine* (Philadelphia: Westminster Press, 1978).
[35]Ibid., 23-25, emphasis added.

themselves compelled to do so as the only rational means of explanation of their experience of God in Christ."[36] Secondly, however, Wiles declares that,

> The "threeness" of the completed orthodox doctrine of the Trinity can logically only be known on the basis of a propositional revelation about the inner mysteries of the Godhead or through some other kind of specific authoritative revelation. If that basis be removed, then the necessity (though not necessarily the desirability or the value) of trinitarian thought is removed.[37]

Lindbeck is critical of Wiles' approach because of its use of the language of intentionality and its lack of historically testable hypotheses.[38] In addition to these criticisms, Wiles seems vulnerable to the critique of analytic philosophy that he has relied upon supposedly objective "facts," which upon consideration seem to be systematically ambiguous.[39] Furthermore, it is ironic that Wiles assumes a propositional view of doctrine in order to refute the possibility of such a view's being able to say anything about God-in-Godself.

In contrast, Lindbeck offers a consistently regulative view of doctrine. Following Wittgenstein, Lindbeck argues that doctrine functions as the "grammar" of the Christian life.[40] The *grammar* of

---

[36]Maurice Wiles, "Some Reflections on the Origins of the Doctrine of the Trinity, " in Maurice Wiles, *Working Papers in Doctrine* (London: SCM Press, 1976) 11. Wiles (ibid.) holds instead that the Fathers "came to accept a trinitarian form because it was the already accepted pattern of expression."

[37]Ibid., 17. John J. O'Donnell has perceptively used Wiles' two alternatives to distinguish respectively between Moltmann's approach to the Trinity ("propositional revelation about the inner mysteries of the Godhead") and that of Schubert Ogden ("some other kind of specific authoritative revelation"), in *Trinity and Temporality: The Christian Doctrine of God in the Light of Process Theology and the Theology of Hope* (Oxford: Oxford University Press, 1983), 146-47.

[38]Lindbeck, *Doctrine*, 109-10, n. 10.

[39]Paul L. Holmer has offered some arguments regarding the ambiguity of "facts" in *The Grammar of Faith* (New York: Harper and Row, 1978), especially 95-107.

[40]See Chapter 2, "Meaning as Use and Theology as Grammar" for further discussion of this theme. The key text in Wittgenstein is *Philosophical Investigations* I: 373.

the Christian faith, as distinguished from its "vocabulary" of "symbols, concepts, rites, injunctions, and stories," underlies and "informs the way the story is told and used."[41] Doctrine shapes the Christian "forms of life" by providing rules as to how Christian language and thought should operate.

In regard to the doctrine of the Trinity and to Christology, Lindbeck offers three examples of rules: "monotheism, historical specificity, and Christological maximalism."[42] Trinitarian doctrine offers "second-order guidelines" for Christian talk about God, rather than binding declarations about the nature of God in God-self. Lindbeck, however, is careful to observe that,

> rule theory does not prohibit speculations on the possible correspondence of the Trinitarian pattern of Christian language to the metaphysical structure of the Godhead, but simply says that these are not doctrinally necessary and cannot be binding.[43]

Thus, in Lindbeck's view, doctrines may be understood as rules that commonly function as "negative guidelines" or boundaries. Doctrines surround but do not claim to explain the mysteries of the faith. Doctrines regulate language about God, not by specifying its content, but by setting the boundaries between "grammatical" and "ungrammatical" speculation.

Childs has offered a helpful assessment of Lindbeck's cultural-linguistic approach from his canonical perspective.[44] Childs' most telling criticism of Lindbeck's approach concerns the inadequacy of "'intratextuality' of meaning . . . as a positive formulation of the Bible's relation to the external world."[45]

As a broadly evangelical theologian, who holds to the unique normativity of Scripture for the Christian faith, I find the application of a strictly regulative view to the Scriptures to be

---

[41]Lindbeck, *Doctrine*, 80-81.

[42]Ibid., 92-96.

[43]Ibid., 106.

[44]Brevard S. Childs, *The New Testament as Canon: An Introduction* (Philadelphia: Fortress Press, 1985), Excursus III, 541-46.

[45]Ibid., 545.

inadequate.[46] The Scriptures are the *norma normans* of the faith, and in this status they are to be distinguished from the *norma normatae* of doctrines. As against propositionalism, the Scriptures are not primarily a collection of Christian doctrines. Rather, they constitute the canon—written traditions, which embody the rule-making rule of faith in an amazing variety of ways.[47]

Nevertheless, when, after beginning with questions of biblical warrants, one turns to questions of the development of doctrine, Lindbeck's regulative perspective seems eminently applicable and useful. For doctrines do indeed function in Christian communities as second-order language about God. Thus, doctrines should be understood as influencing the language that shapes the forms of life of the Christian community. Doctrines may point to the first-order language of the community regarding the Mystery of God and so not be simply and exclusively regulative. Nevertheless, a primary use of the language of doctrine *is* regulative. Applying this regulative function of doctrine to the Trinity leads to a biblical-ly-warranted understanding of God as a Mystery bounded by the "grammatical" language of faith.

· Trinity as Bounded Mystery: Truth in the Tension of Paradox ·

The Trinity and the Incarnation are the two great Mysteries at the center of the Christian faith. "Mystery" is used here in the sense of a truth or reality that is in its depth unfathomable or in its fullness incomprehensible to human understanding. The Mystery will finally be revealed in the eschaton: in this life it can only be partially and fragmentarily known. As Paul declares,

---

[46]See Chapter 1 for further definition and discussion of my own theological perspective, which shapes this argument.

[47]For further discussion of this distinction, see the sections "Scripture and Doctrine: Canon as the Rule of Scripture" and "Scripture and Pattern: Canon and Postcritical Interpretation" in Chapter 4.

For now we see in a mirror, dimly, but then we will see face to face. Now I know only in part; then I will know fully, even as I have been fully known [1 Cor 13:12, *NRSV*].[48]

Given the regulative function of doctrine, the Trinity may be conceived as a Mystery bounded by the "negative guidelines" which have emerged through the historical process of the development of Christian doctrine. How does this view work? How do doctrines provide negative guidelines which bound the Mystery?

The following model of doctrinal exposition contends that both classical and modern understandings of the Trinity set up a field of paradoxical tension.[49] Within this state of paradoxical tension the hermeneutical truth (*coram humanibus*) of the Trinity may be dialectically discerned. Since the Trinity is a continuing Mystery, the hermeneutical truth discovered through this dialectic of paradoxical tension is inevitably fragmentary.

This fragmentary truth is shaped by doctrines that primarily offer "negative guidelines"—rules about how *not* to speak about God. These doctrines function as instantiations of rules, which have the character of "grammar": they provide continuing

---

[48]Although the definition of mystery that I am using is related to the Pauline use of *mysterion* (appearing 21 times in the New Testament), the latter generally carries the positive connotation of a secret now *revealed*, rather than a secret incapable of being fully understood in this life. For the New Testament usage, see Walter Bauer, William F. Arndt, and F. Wilbur Gingrich, ed. and trans., *A Greek-English Lexicon of the New Testament and Other Early Christian Literature* (Chicago: University of Chicago Press, 1957), *ad loc.*

[49]Cf. Kierkegaard's notion of paradox, *Philosophical Fragments*, 46-67. For a critique of the religious use of paradoxical language from the point of view of analytical philosophy, see Ronald W. Hepburn, *Christianity and Paradox* (New York: Pegasus, 1966), especially 16-23. Through the use of "ostensive definition" and "explanatory hypothesis," Hepburn seeks to demonstrate that Christian theological language is hopelessly paradoxical, thus forcing one to embrace a "reluctant agnosticism." The methods Hepburn uses reflect a rather rigid—perhaps even naive—verificational approach to linguistic analysis. Hepburn's arguments fail to consider the ways in which the linguistic analysis of the later Wittgenstein has been used by contemporary Christian philosophers to understand the "grammar" of the language of the Christian faith as a "form of life." See Holmer, *Grammar*, especially ix-xi, 17-36. Also, the section "The Formulation of Postcritical Categories" in Chapter 2 offers further discussion of these themes.

underlying principles that regulate the ways in which faith communities talk about God.[50]

The first major tension that we examine in the historical development of the doctrine of the Trinity is the tension between unity and multiplicity. We will examine this tension in both its classical and modern expressions.

The Tension between Unity and Multiplicity

The plurality and pluriformity of the Scriptural witness to the non-monadic Oneness of God combine with the specifically dyadic and triadic forms of the New Testament to create a biblically-warranted tension between unity and multiplicity in the language about God used by Christian communities. In the Hellenistic cultural setting this tension was augmented by the legacy of the centuries-old pre-Socratic philosophical dispute between the "many" and the "one."[51]

The tension between unity and multiplicity created the matrix in which the doctrine of the Trinity was formed. For it was in the paradoxical assertion of *both* God's "threeness" and God's "oneness" that the concept of "trinity" developed.[52] Both the ancient and modern versions of this tension contribute to a contemporary hermeneutical approach to the Trinity.

---

[50]Cf. Lindbeck, *Doctrine*, 92-96; 108-10, nn. 8 and 10.

[51]For an introduction to the primary sources of this debate see John Mansly Robinson, *An Introduction to Early Greek Philosophy: The Chief Fragments and Ancient Testimony, With Connecting Commentary*, (Boston: Houghton Mifflin, 1968), esp. 87-149. See also G. S. Kirk and J. E. Raven, *The Presocratic Philosophers: A Critical History with a Selection of Texts* (Cambridge: Cambridge Univ. Press, 1982), esp. 182-215 and 263-85. For translations of primary sources from the world of Hellenistic philosophy and critical commentary, see A. A. Long and D. N. Sedley, *The Hellenistic Philosophers*, vol. 1 (New York: Cambridge University Press, 1987).

[52]Although the formal doctrine of the Trinity did not develop until the fourth century, in the context of the Arian controversy, as early as the late second century (c. 180) Theophilus of Antioch uses the Greek term *trias* or "Triad" (*Ad Autolycum* 2:15). In the early third century, Tertullian first used the Latin term *trinitas* (*Adversus Praxean*, 3).

Classical: Modalism and Tritheism. The orthodox leaders of the ancient church, as a result of their long and controversy-ridden struggle in the development of the doctrine of Trinity, concluded that there were two antithetical perils that must be avoided: modalism (or Sabellianism) and tritheism.[53] So, the development of Christian doctrine in this period may be interpreted as providing the negative guidelines that specified that one could not speak "grammatically" (i.e., without heresy) about the Trinity in either of two proscribed ways. On the one hand, the Trinity was not merely three manifestations of the one God; that would reduce the Trinity to theophanies. On the other hand, the Trinity was not three independent gods; that would verge upon polytheism.

Instead, the hermeneutical truth (*coram humanibus*) was contained in the tension between the heretical alternatives that God is monadically one and God is numerically three. The alternatives of modalism and tritheism were not only opposed to one another. They created a field of tension between them, within which the truth may be hermeneutically discerned and (at least partially) appropriated in dialectical fashion.

Modalism and tritheism function something like the ancient Homeric perils of Scylla and Charybdis. Trinitarian speculation naturally and inevitably seemed to "drift" toward one dangerous alternative or the other. For theological reflection on the nature of the Trinity to remain "on course," it had to steer carefully between the twin perils of modalism and tritheism. Such careful and skillful theological "navigation" could only be accomplished if one simultaneously acknowledged the necessity and legitimacy of *both* modalism and tritheism as negative guidelines. Though individually each alternative functioned like an ancient siren—luring the

---

[53]For discussion of the doctrinal significance of various groups and their beliefs, see Bernard Lonergan, *The Way to Nicea: The Dialectical Development of Trinitarian Theology*, trans. Conn O'Donovan (Philadelphia: Westminster Press, 1967). Although there was not a particular group known as the "tritheists" in fourth-century Christianity, this position served as a boundary marker for writers on the Trinity like Gregory of Nyssa (*On "Not Three Gods": To Ablabius*, trans. H. A. Wilson, in *The Nicene and Post-Nicene Fathers*, Series two, vol. 5 [Grand Rapids MI: Eerdmans, originally 1892, reprinted 1962] 331-36).

unwary traveler to destruction—taken together in a relationship of paradoxical tension, they functioned like a modern siren—warning the traveler of danger.[54]

Modern: Psychological and Social. Beginning with Augustine's *On the Trinity* Western Christianity has been both fascinated and frustrated by efforts to ground the Trinity in a human psychological analogy.[55] Rahner favors the possibility of such an analogy, which connects the two processions of the Trinity (Word and Spirit) with the two "basic activities of the Spirit: knowledge and love."[56] Nevertheless, in a terse, severe critique Rahner shows that the Augustinian model is guilty of "circular reasoning." Rather than moving from a model of human psychology to the Trinity, "it postulates *from* the doctrine of the Trinity a model of human knowledge and love."[57]

Rahner proposes a model from a transcendental Thomistic perspective[58] that would incorporate many of the insights of the Augustinian approach into a salvation history understanding of Christian revelation.[59] Instead of using neo-Thomistic epistemology to revise Augustine's psychological analogy, one could better

---

[54]Another traditional metaphor that may perhaps be helpful is that of the lighthouse warning theological "sailors" of the danger of a wreck on the "shoals" of error.

[55]In contemporary Christianity much of this impulse has been carried on through Jungian psychology, which discovers through introspection archetypes of the self that are perhaps analogous to the Augustinian faculties of the self. For example, see W. Harold Grant, Magdala Thompson, and Thomas E. Clarke, *From Image to Likeness: A Jungian Path in the Gospel Journey* (New York: Paulist Press, 1983) and Morton T. Kelsey, *Companions on the Inner Way: The Art of Spiritual Guidance* (New York: Crossroad, 1985).

[56]Rahner, *Trinity*, 116.

[57]Ibid., 117-18.

[58]Cf. Rahner's dissertation on the Thomistic theory of perception, which was failed by Martin Honecker (Karl Rahner, *Geist in Welt*, 2d ed. [Munich: Kösel-Verlag, 1957]).

[59]Rahner, *Trinity*, 119-20.

utilize some contemporary interactional psychological approaches to the self in place of Augustine's outdated faculty psychology.[60]

Like ancient modalism, the psychological analogy of the Trinity becomes heretical when pursued in isolation.[61] Instead, it must be treated in paradoxical tension with its opposite alternative, the social analogy of the Trinity, which displays striking parallels with tritheism.[62] This dynamic relationship between psychological and social analogies creates a field that encourages the exploration of a wide diversity of formulations of the doctrine of the Trinity.

To find a carefully balanced concern with the social nature of the Trinity we will turn to Eastern Orthodoxy. Modern Western views of the Trinity using the social analogy too easily dissolve into tritheism, in contrast to the more cohesive Orthodox views.[63]

In a stimulating article entitled, "The Art of Belonging," Anton Ugolnik reflects upon the significance of the Trinity in contemporary Orthodoxy. As he comments,

> Trinity is an insight into the Inner Life of the Godhead, and a doctrine which banishes any isolationist models of the Self. The contemporary Rumanian Orthodox theologian Dumitru Staniloae . . . promotes a vision of the Spirit as the Quickener of social life in the Church. He structures the life of the Christian mind according to communal principles born in

---

[60]For example, see Ralph H. Turner, "The Self-Concept in Social Interaction," in *The Self in Social Interaction*, ed. Chad Gordon and Kenneth J. Gergen (New York: John Wiley and Sons, 1968), 1: 93-106.

[61]Cf. Rahner's intriguing query at the end of his analysis of the psychological approach: "We might even ask the further question (which we cannot go into here) whether it would not be possible to derive the 'model' for a 'psychological' doctrine of the Trinity not so much from an *abstract* consideration of the human spirit and its activities (in a strangely isolated individualism), but rather from those structures of human existence which first clearly appear in its experience of salvation history" (Rahner, *Trinity*, 119-20).

[62]It is no accident that modern social views of the Trinity drift toward the ancient peril of tritheism. For an example, see Leonard Hodgson, *The Doctrine of the Trinity* (New York: Charles Scribner's Sons, 1944).

[63]Another significant attempt at a counterbalancing view is de Margerie's effort to revive the family analogy of the Trinity (de Margerie, *History*, 274-92). This model seems unsatisfactory due to the logically acceptable but aesthetically incongruous need to liken the *Son* to the maternal figure in the family (Eve) and the *Spirit* (instead of the Son) to the child.

Trinity, rather than in isolating, hierarchical models. The Spirit, in his Orthodox vision, sustains community. . . . Trinity represents the common life inherent in the Godhead. In Staniloae's synthesis, the age-old theological concern with Trinitarian procession, so arcane as to be the object of bitter scorn in more than one contemporary scholar, becomes a paradigm for human interrelationships.[64]

Such a social view of the Trinity clearly stands in tension with the psychological models of the West and their preoccupation with self. For a contemporary understanding of the Trinity, just as for the ancient understanding, the truth is contained in the paradoxical tension. To conceive of God solely with the psychological analogy leads to an isolation that parallels ancient modalism; to conceive of God solely with the social analogy leads to a separation of persons that parallels ancient tritheism. In the paradoxical tension, whether ancient or modern, between unity and multiplicity the truth (*coram humanibus*) of the Mystery of the Trinity is bounded and discovered.

"Already" and "Not Yet"

A second major tension within the Trinity as bounded Mystery is the eschatological tension between God as "already" present and God as "not yet" present. In the New Testament this tension focuses around the theme of the coming of the kingdom of God.[65] As Frank Stagg concludes,

The view that the kingdom of God is present already and the view that the kingdom is yet to come are both securely based in New Testament

---

[64]Anton Ugolnik, "The Art of Belonging," *Religion and Intellectual Life*, 1 (1984): 113-27, at 120.

[65]This tension between present and future may perhaps be rooted in the Old Testament prophets, particularly in an eschatological expectation of the Day of the Lord. This view has been maintained by George Eldon Ladd (*A Theology of the New Testament* [Grand Rapids MI: Eerdmans, 1974] 210), but has been disputed by Gerhard von Rad (*Old Testament Theology*, 2 vols., trans. D. M. G. Stalker [New York: Harper and Row, 1962 and 1965], 2: 112-25).

faith. The harmony of these views is to be found in Jesus Christ himself.[66]

Much contemporary theological reflection upon the doctrine of God is centered upon the question of the relationship between God and temporality.[67] An understanding of the eschatological tension between "already" and "not yet" offers a perspective both for categorizing and criticizing several major approaches to the doctrine of God. Only to the extent that these theologies hold together the "already" and "not yet" aspects of God's presence in paradoxical tension can they claim to have appropriated the richness and balance of the classical understanding of the doctrine of the Trinity.

The God of Propositional Revelation: Already Defined. Scholasticism, whether of the Catholic or Protestant variety, traces its philosophical roots back to the heritage of Aristotle.[68] God is revealed in logical propositions that may be derived with certainty either from the Bible (Protestant scholasticism) or from the teaching office of the Church (Catholic scholasticism). The God of propositional revelation is a God who "already" has been defined. God was present in the past in a definitive, authoritative, and bindingly normative way. The ways in which God is present now and the ways in which God will be present in the future have already been

---

[66]Frank Stagg, *New Testament Theology* (Nashville TN: Broadman Press, 1962) 163. See 149-69 for Stagg's complete discussion of the Kingdom of God. Also, see Ladd, *Theology*, 193-210.

[67]See especially on this issue John J. O'Donnell's lucid book, *Trinity and Temporality*.

[68]For Catholic scholasticism, of course, the pre-eminent figure is Thomas Aquinas, whose utilization of Aristotle is apparent and well-known. (See especially Thomas' philosophical commentaries on Aristotle.) For a perceptive discussion of the hermeneutical dependence of contemporary Protestant scholasticism of the fundamentalist variety upon Aristotelian logic, see the address of William L. Hendricks, "Two Models of Biblical Authority" (Unpublished chapel address, Criswell Center of Biblical Studies, October 15, 1985).

defined. God is unchangeable and clearly perceivable in a strictly rational (factual historical) manner.[69]

Scholastic views downplay the "not yet" aspect of the presence of God, for this is incompatible with clearly defined universal propositions, whether they be in the Latin official theology of the magisterium[70] or in the contemporary evangelical theses of Carl F. H. Henry.[71] In either case, the paradoxical tension between God as already present and God as not yet present has been broken. The "already" has triumphed over the "not yet." Propositional revelation has "already" defined God.

The God of Process Theology: "Not Yet" Defined. Standing in polar opposition to the God of propositional revelation is the God of an experience-based process theology.[72] Rather than being "already" defined, God is "not yet" defined, for in process theology "God's being becomes."[73] The panentheistic God of process theology[74] lacks the capacity to make a clear beginning (creation) and a clear ending (eschatology) in history.[75] Furthermore, the nonhistorical referent of the term "Jesus" tends to reduce Christology purely to existential declarations.[76]

---

[69]Thoughtful scholastics would, of course, not want to limit God's presence to rational human perception of God. Rather propositional revelation clearly defines who God is, and then all of the diverse human experiences of God must conform to or be judged by these propositions in order to be authentic.

[70]H. Denzinger, *Enchiridion Symbolorum Definitionum et Declarationum de Rebus Fidei et Morum*, ed. 33 by A. Schönmetzer (Freiburg i. Br., 1965).

[71]Carl F. H. Henry, *God, Revelation, and Authority*, 6 vols., (Waco TX: Word, 1976) 83.

[72]The argument here is restricted to process theology done from an experiential-expressivist perspective (e.g., Schubert Ogden and John Cobb). Some more recent process theology (e.g., the work of Marjorie Suchoki) has sought to respond to this concern.

[73]O'Donnell, *Temporality*, 87. For O'Donnell's thoughtful analysis of "Trinity and Process," which focuses on the thought of Schubert Ogden, see 53-107.

[74]Cf. here especially Charles Hartshorne's reformulation of Whitehead's "dipolar God" as "the eminent individual" (O'Donnell, *Temporality*, 75-79 and references cited there).

[75]Cf. O'Donnell, *Temporality*, 89.

[76]Ibid., 102-107, for documentation of this criticism and other points of critique.

If the God of propositional theology is too narrowly defined, the God of process theology is too openly defined. For example, O'Donnell argues that for Schubert Ogden "the scriptural symbols of Father, Son, and Holy Spirit are essentially ambiguous and do not form a precise trinity."[77] Instead, the Trinity rests upon the claim that "revelation itself involves an essential three-foldness."[78] God and the world have become "correlative terms."[79] The tension between God and the world portrayed in Scripture has been greatly reduced, as God is understood as a dependent and correlative dimension of the world.[80] The Trinity—in particular, the economic Trinity—has been dissolved "in the process."

The God of Eschatological Theology: Defined in the Death of God. Between the already defined God of propositional theology and the not yet defined God of process theology, one can locate the God of contemporary eschatological theology. Theologians, such as Jürgen Moltmann[81] and Eberhard Jüngel,[82] who occupy this

---

[77]Ibid., 85.

[78]Ibid.

[79]Ibid., 89. On this central aspect of process theology, see especially the final chapter of Whitehead's *Process and Reality*, which is entitled "God and the World" (Alfred North Whitehead, *Process and Reality: An Essay in Cosmology* [New York: Macmillan, 1929], 519-33). Also, see John B. Cobb, Jr., *God and the World* (Philadelphia: Westminster Press, 1969).

[80]Note, for example, the contrasting uses of *kosmos* in the New Testament— from the world that God loves to the world that God hates. For a comprehensive listing of usages see Bauer, Arndt, and Gingrich, *Lexicon, ad loc.*, especially contrasting sense 4c ("all [hu]mankind, but especially of believers, as the object of God's love") and sense 7 ("the world, and everything that belongs to it appears as that which is at enmity w[ith] God, i.e. lost in sin, wholly at odds w[ith] anything divine, ruined and depraved").

[81]Jürgen Moltmann, *The Trinity and the Kingdom: The Doctrine of God*, trans. Margaret Kohl (San Francisco: Harper and Row, 1981).

[82]Eberhard Jüngel, *God as the Mystery of the World: On the Foundation of the Theology of the Crucified One in the Dispute between Theism and Atheism*, trans. Darrell L. Guder (Grand Rapids MI: Eerdmans, 1983).

intermediate position, reflect in their theology the eschatological tension between the "already" and the "not yet."[83]

Eschatological theologians are particularly concerned to respond to the problem of "death of God" talk in the late twentieth century. One common approach to the problem is expressed in attempts to fuse Karl Barth's christocentric perspective on all Christian doctrine[84] with Bonhoeffer's "religionless Christianity."[85] The philosophical renewal of language about the death of God reflects the development of a "protest atheism,"[86] which derives from the perceived collapse of the metaphysical God of classical theism.[87] Eschatological theology tries to absorb the reality of the experience of the death of God by identifying the death of God with the Crucifixion.[88] Thus, in a fashion reminiscent of the New Testament treatment of the eschatological paradox,[89] the Crucified One becomes the focus for the "already" and "not yet." One dialectically identifies with God *both* in God's presence and in God's absence.[90]

---

[83]For a helpful typology showing the relationship of this intermediate position to the views of classical theism and process theology, see O'Donnell *Temporality*, 86-89 (cf. also 130-33 on Moltmann).

[84]Cf., for example, Karl Barth *Church Dogmatics*, I: 1, chap. 1, "The Word of God as the Criterion of Dogmatics," 51-335, especially 124-35.

[85]Dietrich Bonhoeffer, *Letters and Papers from Prison*, enlarged edition, ed. Eberhard Bethge (New York: Macmillan, 1971), 324-63. Also, see especially Jüngel's analysis of "Bonhoeffers's Contribution to the Return of the 'Death of God' Talk to Theology" (*Mystery*, 57-63).

[86]O'Donnell, *Temporality*, 7-11, 17-21. Cf. Moltmann, *Trinity*, 48.

[87]Also, as O'Donnell clearly demonstrates, the rise of "protest atheism" is intimately related to post-Holocaust struggles with the problem of suffering. The following section of this chapter attempts directly, though briefly, to deal with the relationship between the question of suffering and the doctrine of God.

[88]Luther's theology of the cross is cited as historical precedent for this move. See especially Jürgen Moltmann, *The Crucified God*, trans. R. A. Wilson and John Bowden (New York: Harper and Row, 1974).

[89]See the quotation by Frank Stagg (*Theology*, 163) cited in the introduction to this chapter's discussion of " 'Already' and 'Not Yet.' "

[90]As Jüngel maintains, "But God's presence can only be experienced simultaneously with his absence" (*Mystery*, 104; cf. also 54-55, 62-63, 165-66).

The eschatological theologians, to a far greater degree than either their propositionalist or process colleagues, manage to preserve the tension inherent in the "already" and the "not yet" in the doctrine of God. Yet their staurological concentration and their appropriation of death-of-God language raises a haunting suspicion. Exactly what is the philosophical status of the God whose "being is in becoming" (Jüngel)[91] and who will fulfill human desire for God's presence only in the eschatological future (Moltmann)?[92]

To express the concern more directly, is it possible that the sophisticated dialectical, future-oriented language of eschatological theologians concerning the topic of the death of God is finally an elaborate psycholinguistic illusion? These theologians need to respond more specifically to the charge that their language about God is just the projection into the future of an illusion. In their zeal to deal completely and effectively with Feuerbach and Nietzsche,[93] have they responded adequately to the critique of Freud?[94]

Although each of the options we have discussed legitimately seeks to balance the tension between God as "already" present and God as "not yet" present, no perfect balance exists. A canonical approach to doctrine seeks to locate each view within the biblically-initiated matrix of tensions in the historical development of the doctrine of God.

Power and Goodness

A third major tension within the Trinity as bounded Mystery is the paradoxical tension between God's power and God's goodness. Suffering—especially innocent suffering—in its relationship to the

---

[91]Jüngel, *Mystery*, 159, 380-89.

[92]Moltmann, *Trinity*, 49.

[93]Jüngel, *Mystery*, especially 98-100, 141-52, 203-13, 334-43. Jürgen Moltmann, *Theology of Hope: On the Ground and Implications of a Christian Eschatology*, trans. James W. Leitch (New York: Harper and Row, 1967), 170-72 and *passim*.

[94]See especially Sigmund Freud, *The Future of an Illusion*, trans. W. D. Robson-Scott, rev. and ed. James Strachey (Garden City NY: Doubleday, 1964).

nature of God is the basic issue here.[95] As the traditional question of theodicy exclaims, "How can a good and omnipotent God allow such unjust suffering in the world?"[96]

The tension between God's power and goodness, like the tensions between unity and multiplicity and "already" and "not yet," which we have previously examined, contains the truth (*coram humanibus*) within the paradox. To attempt to resolve the problem by embracing either one of the alternatives that bound the mystery is rashly to cut the Gordian knot. Such simple resolutions result in speaking heretically, rather than "grammatically" about the Mystery of God.

Those who attempt to resolve the question by holding to the power of God while compromising God's goodness are driven either to the expedient of dualism or the alternative of a universe ruled by an all-powerful, malevolent God.[97] Since the days of Marcion, the Christian church has clearly declared that dualistic thinking violates the oneness of God, while the malevolent God verges upon the demonic.

The opposite response to the question of theodicy is far more commonly found in contemporary discussion, especially of a popular nature. It attempts to resolve the problem of suffering by holding to the goodness of God while compromising God's power.[98]

---

[95]As Moltmann observes, "The question about God and the question about suffering are a joint, a common question. And they only find a common answer. Either that, or neither of them finds a satisfactory answer at all" (*Trinity*, 49).

[96]The perennial popular interest in this question is perhaps most clearly epitomized by Rabbi Harold S. Kushner's best-selling book, *When Bad Things Happen to Good People* (New York: Avon, 1981). A useful survey of the issue from a philosophical-historical perspective is John Hick, *Evil and the God of Love*, rev. ed. (San Francisco: Harper and Row, 1978). Hick advocates an "Irenaean theodicy," which combines a developmental moral view with an eschatological grounding, in contrast to the classic Augustinian theodicy (especially 236-40). For a lively discussion of some contemporary options, see Stephen T. Davis, ed., *Encountering Evil: Live Options in Theodicy* (Atlanta: John Knox Press, 1981).

[97]For example, see the essays in Davis, *Encountering Evil* by John K. Roth (7-22) and Frederick Sontag (137-51).

[98]This is the response of Kushner's autobiographical approach (*Bad Things*, especially 113-31) and S. Paul Schilling's much more theologically sophisticated *God and Human Anguish* (Nashville TN: Abingdon, 1977), especially 236-48. Many

Perhaps such a view may be defended as a compassionate pastoral response to persons who experience distance from an all-powerful God in the powerlessness of their suffering.[99] Neverthless, by limiting God's power, this approach reduces the tension inherent in biblical portrayals of God and suffering.[100]

A more theologically balanced approach is offered by Moltmann, who seeks to ground both the Christian doctrine of God and the Christian response to suffering in the event of the cross.[101] As O'Donnell has demonstrated, however, serious problems are raised by such a focus upon the crucifixion as *the* criterion for the doctrine of God.[102] The most significant of these derives from Moltmann's double use of *paradidomi* (Rom 8:32, Gal 2:20) as the exegetical warrant for the relationship between the Father and the Son.[103] Not only does this view of the relationship between the cross and the Trinity raise the questions of subordinationism and possible tritheism, but finally it makes God appear as "the executioner."[104] Moreover, this view ignores or downplays other

---

treatments of theodicy within the framework of process theology fall into this category as well (e.g., the process theodicy of John Cobb).

[99]This is an important theme in much contemporary pastoral theology. For example, see James Newton Poling, *The Abuse of Power: A Theological Problem* (Nashville TN: Abingdon, 1991).

[100]The classic example of this tension-bounded mystery is the book of Job, particularly God's response in chapters 38-41.

[101]Moltmann, *Crucified God*; also, Moltmann, "God and Suffering," *Trinity*, 47-52. O'Donnell's analysis of Moltmann's *The Crucified God* is most helpful here (*Temporality*, 108-20).

[102]O'Donnell, *Temporality*, 147-56. Another illuminating study which seeks to utilize and correct both Moltmann and process thought is Paul S. Fiddes, *The Creative Suffering of God* (Oxford: Clarendon Press, 1988).

[103]"The Father delivers up the Son and the Son delivers up himself in obedience to the Father's will" (O'Donnell, *Temporality*, 119).

[104]O'Donnell, *Temporality*, 153-56. Dorothee Sölle initially voiced this criticism in "Gott und das Leiden," in *Diskussion über Jürgen Moltmanns Buch "Der Gekreuzigte Gott,"* ed. Michale Welker (Munich: Kaiser, 1979).

elements in the Father-Son relationship that are not directly related to the Passion.[105]

Another insightful contemporary discussion that grounds the problem of suffering in the doctrine of the Trinity is that of Arthur McGill.[106] McGill argues that the historical development of the doctrine of the Trinity contains a key insight into the theological problem of suffering. Specifically, McGill claims that the Arian controversy demonstrates that the essential mark of God's divinity is the act of self-giving, which is grounded in the mutual self-giving of the Father and the Son.[107] Perhaps the notion of self-giving (cf. *kenosis*) can avoid some of the problems of Moltmann's "delivering up" notion, which frequently is rendered as "betrayal" in the New Testament.[108]

By understanding the problem of suffering in light of the inner-trinitarian relation of love between the Father and the Son, McGill rules out accusations of "God the executioner." The weakness of McGill's view, unfortunately, is the same one that Augustine discovered in his own view of the Trinity as lover, beloved, and the bond of love: viz., "it does not seem to follow, therefore, that whenever there is love, three things must be understood."[109]

Both the incomprehensibility of suffering and the incomprehensibility of the God who is bounded in the paradoxical tension of power and goodness point beyond reason towards

---

[105]I am particularly indebted to William Hendricks for this point. See also Fiddes, *Creative Suffering*. This criticism may perhaps be more generally extended to eschatological theology.

[106]Arthur C. McGill, *Suffering: A Test of Theological Method* (Philadelphia: Westminster Press, 1982), especially 64-82.

[107]For an alternative view of the Arian controversy which emphasizes *Arius'* soteriological concern, see Maurice Wiles' essays, "In Defense of Arius" and "The Doctrine of Christ in the Patristic Age," in Wiles, *Working Papers*, 28-49.

[108]Matt 26:25,46,48; Mark 14:42,44; Luke 22:21; John 13:11; 18:2,5. See Bauer, Arndt, and Gingrich, *Lexicon, ad loc*. O'Donnell's suggestion that Moltmann reply to Sölle's objection by "a fuller trinitarian development of the double surrender of Father and Son" (*Temporality*, 154-55) points in the same general direction as McGill. McGill's notion of self-giving, however, seems to be more in the spirit of the classical Johannine passages describing the relation between the Father and the Son.

[109]*De Trinitate*, IX: 2. *The Trinity*, McKenna trans. 272.

Mystery. This is perhaps the place where theological thought reaches its own limiting boundary. Christians are finally forced to realize that their most sophisticated thinking and speech is ultimately nothing more than stuttering in the face of the great Mystery of God.[110]

· Canon as Musical Praise ·

Holy, holy, holy! Lord God Almighty!
All Thy works shall praise Thy name
    in earth, and sky, and sea;
Holy, holy, holy; merciful and mighty!
God in three Persons, blessed Trinity![111]

A canonical model of the doctrine of God ends in musical doxology. The canon of Scripture is transmuted into a canon of praise. Augustine glimpsed this vision when he described the "order of the ages" as a "most beautiful song" or "exquisite poem."[112]

In the face of the ineffable Mystery of God, persons of faith are at last either reduced to silent contemplation or called to grateful praise. The bounded Mystery of the Trinity is finally to be celebrated or contemplated, rather than explained. In its worship the Christian church has primarily chosen the way of celebration. As Wainwright reminds Christian theologians, "It is in and

---

[110]Cf. Job 38-41; Isa 55:8-9.

[111]Reginald Heber, "Holy, Holy, Holy," 1826, stanza 4.

[112]Augustine, *City of God*, XI: 18, as found in Saint Augustine, *The City of God Against the Pagans*, trans. David S. Wiesen, The Loeb Classical Library (Cambridge MA: Harvard Univ. Press, 1968), 3: 494-95. The Latin text reads: "atque ita ordinem saeculorum tamquam pulcherrimum carmen etiam ex quibusdam quasi antithetis honestaret." I prefer the more literal translation "most beautiful song" to Wiesen's "exquisite poem." I am indebted to H. I. Marrou (*Time and Timeliness*, trans. Violet Neville [New York: Sheed & Ward, 1969] 71ff.) for pointing out this analogy. Marrou also cites Augustine's *Epistles* 138: 1 [5] and 166, 5 [13] as examples.

through the worshiping community that most believers catch the Christian vision."[113]

Thus, the ancient tradition of *singing* the Creed—found occasionally in Catholic settings (e.g., high mass, monastic communities) and preserved regularly in Orthodoxy—has far more to commend it than mere custom. For in celebration of the Mystery of the Trinity in song one has the opportunity to appropriate its reality in a new way. Singing, rather than doctrinal recital, affords a more comprehensive way of "confessing" the truth of the faith. The process of singing unites both thought and action. Like confession and prayer, singing is a joint expression of the mind and the heart.[114]

The celebration of the Trinity in a canon of praise offers a way to transcend the logical limitations of theological and philosophical language in expressing the Mystery of God. In song the alternatives of paradox need not be denied or analyzed but can be poetically juxtaposed. As Augustine observes, God's most beautiful song is "enhanced by what might be called antitheses."[115] Thus, the bounded Mystery of the Trinity may be more clearly perceived spiritually—as a reality appropriated in but not limited to space and time. Such perception must be criticized and guided by

---

[113]Wainwright, *Doxology*, 435.

[114]Cf. the following definition of spiritual prayer by the Russian Orthodox Bishop Theophan the Recluse (1815-1894): "Prayer is the raising of the *mind and heart* to God in praise and thanksgiving to Him and in supplication for the good things we need, both spiritual and physical. The essence of prayer is therefore the spiritual lifting of the heart towards God. The *mind in the heart* stands consciously before the face of God, filled with due reverence, and begins to pour itself out before Him" (Theophan the Recluse, "What Is Prayer?" in *The Art of Prayer*, compiled Igumen Chariton of Valamo, trans. E. Kadloubovsky and E. M. Palmer, ed. Timothy Ware [London: Faber and Faber, 1966] 53, emphasis added).

[115]Augustine, *City of God*, XI: 18. See note 112 for the Latin context of Augustine's use of *antithetis*. In this chapter Augustine makes use of 2 Cor 6:7-10 and Ecclus 33:14-15 as biblical illustrations of the use of antithesis in language. I am, of course, seeking to appropriate Augustine's use of antithesis in language here without adopting the Neoplatonic philosophy which shapes his worldview. Modern surrealist art, for example, offers a contemporary visual example utilizing the juxtaposition of opposites without dependence upon ancient philosophy or metaphysics.

theological reflection in order to avoid the ever-present possibilities of self-deception, illusion, and the bewitchment of being.

The possibility of singing the doctrine of the Trinity calls us beyond the limits of human logic and the inadequacies of human language to affirm and celebrate the great and marvelous mystery of the Triune God.

> Gloria patri et filio et spiritui sancto, sicut erat in principio, et nunc et semper et in saecula saeculorum.[116] Amen.

---

[116]"Glory be to the Father, and to the Son, and to the Holy Ghost; as it was in the beginning, is now and ever shall be, world without end."

BIBLIOGRAPHY

Ahlstrom, Sydney. *Theology in America: The Major Voices from Puritanism to Neo-Orthodoxy*. Indianapolis IN: Bobbs-Merrill, 1967.

Allen, Diogenes. *Christian Belief in a Postmodern World: The Full Wealth of Conviction*. Louisville KY: Westminster/John Knox Press, 1989.

Augustine, *De Trinitate*. E. T. Saint Augustine, *The Trinity*. Trans. Stephen McKenna. *The Fathers of the Church*, Vol. 45, Washington DC: Catholic University of America Press, 1963.

————. *De Civitate Dei Contra Paganos*. E.T. Saint Augustine, *The City of God Against the Pagans*. Trans. David S. Wiesen. The Loeb Classical Library. Cambridge MA: Harvard University Press, 1968, Vol. III.

Baillie, John. *The Idea of Revelation in Recent Thought*. New York: Columbia University Press, 1956.

Barr, James. *The Bible in the Modern World*. London: SCM Press, 1973.

————. "Childs' Introduction to the Old Testament as Scripture." *Journal for the Study of the Old Testament* 16 (1980): 12-23.

————. *Escaping From Fundamentalism*. London: SCM Press, 1984.

————. *Fundamentalism*. London: SCM Press, 1977.

————. *Holy Scripture: Canon, Authority, Criticism*. Oxford: Oxford University Press, 1983.

————. *Old and New in Interpretation: A Study of the Two Testaments*. London: SCM Press, 1966.

————. *The Semantics of Biblical Language*. Oxford: Oxford University Press, 1961.

Barth, Karl. *Die Kirchliche Dogmatik*. 13 vols. and index vol. Zollikon: Verlag der Evangelischen Buchhandlung, 1932–1970. E. T. *Church Dogmatics*. Trans. Geoffrey Bromiley *et al*. Edinburgh: T. and T. Clark, 1955–1977.

Barton, John. *Oracles of God: Perceptions of Ancient Prophecy in Israel after the Exile*. New York: Oxford University Press, 1986.

————. *People of the Book? The Authority of the Bible in Christianity*. London: SPCK, 1988.

————. *Reading the Old Testament: Method in Biblical Study*. London: Darton, Longman, and Todd, 1984.

Benoit, Pierre. "Revelation et Inspiration," *Revue Biblique* 70 (1963), 321-70.

Bleicher, Josef. *Contemporary Hermeneutics: Hermeneutics as Method, Philosophy and Critique*. Boston: Routledge and Kegan Paul, 1980.

Bloch, Renee. "Midrash." *Approaches to Ancient Judaism: Theory and Practice.* Trans. Mary Howard Callaway. Ed. William Scott Green. Missoula MT: Scholars Press, 1978, 29-50.

Blondel, Maurice. *The Letter on Apologetics and History and Dogma.* Trans. Alexander Dru and Illtyd Trethowan. London: Harvill Press, 1964.

Bonhöffer, Dietrich. *Letters and Papers from Prison.* Enlarged edition. Ed. Eberhard Bethge. New York: Macmillan, 1971.

Brett, Mark G. *Biblical Criticism in Crisis? The Impact of the Canonical Approach upon Old Testament Studies.* New York: Cambridge University Press, 1991.

Brown, Raymond E. *Biblical Exegesis and Church Doctrine.* London: Geoffrey Chapman, 1985.

Brunner, Emil. *Truth as Encounter.* Trans. Amandus W. Loos and David Cairns. Philadelphia: Westminster Press, 1964.

Bubner, R., K. Cramer, and R. Wiehl. *Hermeneutik und Dialektik: Aufsatze.* 2 vols. Tubingen: J. C. B. Mohr, 1970.

Calvin, John. *Institutes of the Christian Religion.* 2 vols. Trans. Ford Lewis Battles. Ed. John T. McNeill. London: SCM Press, 1981.

Carr, Edward Hallett. *What Is History?* New York: Random House (Vintage), 1961.

Childs, Brevard S. *Biblical Theology in Crisis.* Philadelphia: Westminster Press, 1970.

_____. *Biblical Theology of the Old and New Testaments: Theological Reflection on the Christian Bible.* Philadelphia: Fortress Press, 1993.

_____. *The Book of Excdus: A Critical, Theological Commentary.* The Old Testament Library. Philadelphia: Westminister Press, 1974; also London: SCM Press, 1974.

_____. "The Canonical Shape of the Prophetic Literature." *Interpretation* 32 (1978): 46-55.

_____. "The Exegetical Significance of Canon for the Study of the Old Testament." Ninth IOSOT *Congress Volume,* Gottingen, 1977. Ed. J. A. Emerton *et al. Supplement to Vetus Testamentum* 29. Leiden: Brill, 1978, 66-80.

_____. "Gerhard von Rad in American Dress." *The Hermeneutical Quest: Essays in Honor of James Luther Mays on His Sixty-Fifth Birthday.* Allison Park PA: Pickwick Publications, 1986.

_____. *Introduction to the Old Testament as Scripture.* Philadelphia: Fortress Press, 1979; also London: SCM Press, 1979.

_____. *Memory and Tradition in Israel.* Studies in Biblical Theology 37. Naperville IL: Alec R. Allenson, 1962; also London: SCM Press, 1962.

_____. "Midrash and the Old Testament." *Understanding the Sacred Text: Essays in Honor of Morton S. Enslin on the Hebrew Bible and Christian Beginnings*. Ed. J. Reumann. Valley Forge PA: Judson Press, 1972.

_____. *Myth and Reality in the Old Testament*. Studies in Biblical Theology 27. Naperville IL: Alec R. Allenson, 1960; also London: SCM Press, 1960.

_____. *The New Testament as Canon: An Introduction*. Philadelphia: Fortress Press, 1985; also London: SCM Press, 1985.

_____. "The Old Testament as Scripture of the Church." *Concordia Theological Monthly* 43 (1972): 709-22.

_____. *Old Testament Theology in a Canonical Context*. Philadelphia: Fortress Press, 1986; also London: SCM Press, 1986.

_____. "On Reading the Elijah Narratives." *Interpretation* 34 (1980): 128-37.

_____. "Psalm 8 in the Context of the Christian Canon." *Interpretation* 23 (1969): 20-31.

_____. "A Response." *Horizons in Biblical Theology* 2 (1980): 199-211.

_____. "Response to Reviewers of *Introduction to the Old Testament as Scripture*." *Journal for the Study of the Old Testament* 16 (1980): 52-60.

_____. Review of *Holy Scripture: Canon, Authority, Criticism*, by James Barr. *Interpretation* 38 (1984): 66-70.

_____. "A Traditio-historical Study of the Reed Sea Tradition." *Vetus Testamentum* 20 (1970): 406-18.

Cobb, John B., Jr. *God and the World*. Philadelphia: Westminster Press, 1969.

Copleston, Frederick. "Kant." *A History of Philosophy*. Vol. 6, Part II. Garden City NY: Doubleday (Image), 1964.

Creed, John Martin. *The Divinity of Jesus Christ: A Study in the History of Christian Doctrine Since Kant*. Cambridge: Cambridge University Press, 1938.

Creegan, Charles L. *Wittgenstein and Kierkegaard: Religion, Individuality, and Philosophical Method*. London: Routledge, 1989.

Croatto, J. Severino. *Biblical Hermeneutics: Toward a Theory of Reading as the Production of Meaning*. Trans. Robert R. Barr. Maryknoll NY: Orbis, 1987.

Culpepper, R. Alan. *Anatomy of the Fourth Gospel: A Study of Literary Design*. Philadelphia: Fortress Press, 1983.

Davie, Ian. *A Theology of Speech: An Essay in Philosophical Theology*. London: Sheed and Ward, 1973.

Davis, Stephen T. *Encountering Evil: Live Options in Theodicy*. Atlanta: John Knox Press, 1981.

de Lubac, Henri. *Exegese medievale: Le quatre sens de l'Ecriture.* 2 vols. in 4. Paris: Aubier, 1959-64.

de Margerie, Bertrand. *The Christian Trinity in History.* Trans. Edmund J. Fortman. Still River MA: St. Bede's, 1982.

Denzinger, H. *Enchiridion Symbolorum Definitionum et Declarationum de Rebus Fidei et Morum.* Editio 33 by A. Schonmetzer. (Freiburg i. Br., 1965).

Descartes, Rene. *Discourse on Method and the Meditations.* Trans. F. E. Sutcliffe. Harmondsworth: Penguin Books, 1968.

Dilschneider, Otto. *Gegenwart Christi: Grundriss einer Dogmatik der Offenbarung.* 2 vols. Gutersloh: C. Bartelsmann Verlag, 1948.

Donovan, Peter. *Religious Language.* New York: Hawthorn Books, 1976.

Downing, F. Gerald. *Has Christianity a Revelation?* Philadelphia: Westminster Press, 1964.

Drury, John. Review of *The New Testament as Canon: An Introduction. Theology* 89 (1986): 60-62.

Dulles, Avery. *Models of Revelation.* Dublin: Gill and Macmillan, 1983.

_____. *Revelation Theology: A History.* New York: Herder and Herder, 1969.

_____. "The Theology of Revelation." *Theological Studies* 25 (1964): 43-58.

Ebeling, Gerhard. "Erwagungen zu einer evangelischen Fundamentaltheologie." *Zeitschrift fur Theologie und Kirche* 67 (1970): 479-524.

_____. *The Word of God and Tradition: Historical Studies Interpreting the Divisions of Christianity.* Trans. S. H. Hooke. London: Collins, 1968.

Fackre, Gabriel. *The Christian Story: A Pastoral Systematics.* Vol. 2. *Authority: Scripture in the Church for the World.* Grand Rapids MI: Eerdmans, 1987.

Fairweather, A. M. *The Word as Truth: A Critical Examination of the Christian Doctrine of Revelation in the Writings of Thomas Aquinas and Karl Barth.* London: Lutterworth Press, 1944.

Farrer, Austin. *The Glass of Vision.* London: Dacre Press, 1948.

Fernandez, Domiciano. "Concepto de revelacion." *Revista Espanola de Teologia* 24 (1964): 3-36.

Ferré, Frederick. *Language, Logic, and God.* London: Eyre and Spottiswood, 1962.

Fiddes, Paul S. *The Creative Suffering of God.* Oxford: Clarendon Press, 1988.

Florovsky, Georges. *Bible, Church, Tradition: An Eastern Orthodox View.* Vol. I of *Collected Works.* Belmont MA: Nordland, 1972.

_____. "Revelation, Philosophy, and Theology." Trans. Richard Haugh. *Creation and Redemption.* Vol. 3 of *The Collected Works.* Belmont MA: Nordland, 1976.

Forsyth, P. T. *The Principle of Authority in Relation to Certainty, Sanctity and Society: An Essay in the Philosophy of Experimental Religion.* London: Hodder and Stoughton, 1912.

Frei, Hans W. "An Afterword: Eberhard Busch's Biography of Karl Barth." *Karl Barth In Re-View: Posthumous Works Reviewed and Assessed.* Ed. H. Martin Rumscheidt. Pittsburg PA: Pickwick Press, 1981, 95-116.

_____. *The Eclipse of Biblical Narrative: A Study in Eighteenth and Nineteenth Century Hermeneutics.* New Haven CT: Yale University Press, 1974.

Freud, Sigmund. *The Future of an Illusion.* Trans. W. D. Robson-Scott. Rev. and ed. James Strachey. Garden City NY: Doubleday, 1964.

Frye, Northrop. *The Great Code: The Bible and Literature.* New York: Harcourt, Brace and Jovanovich, 1982.

Gadamer, Hans-Georg. *Philosophical Hermeneutics.* Trans. David E. Linge. Berkeley: University of California Press, 1976.

_____. *Wahrheit und Methode.* 2d ed. Tubingen: J. C. B. Mohr, 1965. E. T. *Truth and Method.* Ed. Garrett Barden and John Cumming. New York: Seabury Press, 1975.

George, Timothy. *John Robinson and the English Separatist Tradition.* Macon GA: Mercer University Press, 1982.

Gartner, Bertil. *The Areopagus Speech and Natural Revelation.* Trans. Carolyn Hanney King. Uppsala: Almquist and Wiksells, 1955.

Grant, Robert M., with David Tracy. *A Short History of the Interpretation of the Bible.* 2d ed. Philadelphia: Fortress Press, 1984.

Grant, W. Harold, Magdala Thompson, and Thomas E. Clarke. *From Image to Likeness: A Jungian Path in the Gospel Journey.* New York: Paulist Press, 1983.

Green, Garrett. "The Bible As . . . : Fictional Narrative and Scriptural Truth." *Scriptural Authority and Narrative Interpretation.* Ed. Garret Green. Philadelphia: Fortress Press, 1987, 79-96.

Gregory of Nyssa. *On "Not Three Gods": To Ablabius.* Trans. H. A. Wilson. *The Nicene and Post-Nicene Fathers,* Series Two, Vol. 5. Ed. Henry Wace. Grand Rapids MI: Eerdmans, 1892; rpt. 1952, 331-36.

Guardini, Romano. *Religion und Offenbarung.* Wurzburg: Werkbund Verlag, 1958.

Gutierrez, Gustavo. *A Theology of Liberation.* Rev. ed. Trans. and ed. by Caridad Inda and John Eagleson. Maryknoll NY: Orbis, 1988.

Habermas, Jurgen. "The Hermeneutic Claim to Universality." Trans. Josef Bleicher. *Contemporary Hermeneutics: Hermeneutics as Method, Philosophy and Critique.* Boston: Routledge and Kegan Paul, 1980, 181-211.

Hegel, G. W. F. *The Phenomenology of Mind.* 2d ed. rev. Trans. J. Baillie. London: George Allan and Unwin, 1949.

Hendricks, William L. "Revelatory Implicates of the Threefoldness of God." Unpublished lecture, The Southern Baptist Theological Seminary, September 4, 1985.

Hendricks, William L. "Two Models of Biblical Authority." Chapel Address presented at Criswell Center of Biblical Studies (October 15, 1985).

Henry, Carl F. H. *God, Revelation, and Authority,* 6 vols. Waco TX: Word, 1976-1983.

Hepburn, Ronald W. *Christianity and Paradox.* New York: Pegasus, 1966.

Herzog, Frederick. *God-Walk: Liberation Shaping Dogmatics.* Maryknoll NY: Orbis, 1988.

Hick, John. *Evil and the God of Love.* Rev. ed. San Francisco: Harper and Row, 1978.

High, Dallas M., ed. *New Essays on Religious Language.* New York: Oxford University Press, 1969.

Hodge, Charles. *Systematic Theology,* 3 vols. New York: Charles Scribner's Sons, 1872.

Hodgson, Leonard. *The Doctrine of the Trinity.* New York: Charles Scribner's Sons, 1944

Holmer, Paul L. *The Grammar of Faith.* San Francisco: Harper and Row, 1978.

Hoy, David Couzens. *The Critical Circle: Literature, History, and Philosophical Hermeneutics.* Berkeley: University of California Press, 1978.

Hudson, W. Donald. *Wittgenstein and Religious Belief.* London: Macmillan, 1975.

Hunter, J. F. M. " 'Forms of Life' in Wittgenstein's *Philosophical Investigations.*" *American Philosophical Quarterly* 5 (1968): 233-43.

Jedin, Hubert. *A History of the Council of Trent.* 2 vols. Trans. Dom Ernest Graf. New York: Thomas Nelson, 1957, 1961.

Johnson, Robert Clyde. "Christian Doctrine II." Unpublished lectures, Yale University Divinity School, 1975.

Josephus, *Contra Apionem/Against Apion.* Trans. H. St. J. Thackeray. Loeb Classical Library. Cambridge MA: Harvard University Press, 1961.

Jungel, Eberhard. *God as the Mystery of the World: On the Foundation of the Theology of the Crucified One in the Dispute between Theism and Atheism.* Trans. Darrell L. Guder. Grand Rapids MI: Eerdmans, 1983.

Kant, Immanuel. *Critique of Pure Reason*. Trans. J. M. D. Meiklejohn. London: George Bell and Sons, 1901.

Keightley, Alan. *Wittgenstein, Grammar and God*. London: Epworth Press, 1976.

Kelly, J. N. D. *Early Christian Doctrines*. 2d ed. New York: Harper and Row, 1960.

Kelsey, David H. *The Uses of Scripture in Recent Theology*. Philadelphia: Fortress Press, 1975.

Kelsey, Morton T. *Companions on the Inner Way: The Art of Spiritual Guidance*. New York: Crossroad, 1985.

Kenny, Anthony. *The Legacy of Wittgenstein*. Oxford: Basil Blackwell, 1984.

_____. *Wittgenstein*. London: Penguin, 1973.

Kerr, Fergus. *Theology after Wittgenstein*. Oxford: Basil Blackwell, 1986.

Kierkegaard, Søren. *Concluding Unscientific Postscript*. Trans. David F. Swenson and Walter Lowrie. Princeton: Princeton University Press, 1941.

_____. *Philosophical Fragments or A Fragment of Philosophy*. 2d ed. Trans. David Swenson and Howard Hong. Princeton: Princeton University Press, 1962.

_____. *Training in Christianity*. Trans. Walter Lowrie. Princeton: Princeton University Press, 1967, c. 1941.

Kirk, G. S., and J. E. Raven. *The Presocratic Philosophers: A Critical History with a Selection of Texts*. Cambridge: Cambridge University Press, 1982.

Kliever, Lonnie D. *The Shattered Spectrum: A Survey of Contemporary Theology*. Richmond: John Knox Press, 1981.

Kung, Hans. *Justification: The Doctrine of Karl Barth and a Catholic Reflection*. Expanded edition. Philadelphia: Westminster, 1981.

Kushner, Harold S. *When Bad Things Happen to Good People*. New York: Avon, 1981.

Ladd, George Eldon. *A Theology of the New Testament*. Grand Rapids MI: Eerdmans, 1974.

Lash, Nicholas. "How Large is a 'Language Game'?" *Theology* 87 (1984): 19-28.

Latourelle, Rene. *Theologie de la Revelation*. 2d. ed. Bruges: Desclee de Brouwer, 1966.

Latourelle, Rene, and Gerald O'Collins. *Problems and Perspectives of Fundamental Theology*. Trans. Matthew J. O'Connell. New York: Paulist Press, 1982. Originally published as *Problemi e Prospective di Teologia Fondamentale*. Rome: Editrice Queriniana, 1980.

Leiman, Sid Z. *The Canonization of Hebrew Scripture: The Talmudic and Midrashic Evidence.* Hamden CT: Archon Books, 1976.

_____. "Inspiration and Canonicity: Reflections on the Formation of the Biblical Canon." *Jewish and Christian Self-Definition* II. Ed. E. P. Sanders. Philadelphia: Fortress Press, 1981, 56-63, 316-18.

Lewis, H. D. "Revelation Without Content." *The Hibbert Journal* 48 (1950): 379-82.

Lindbeck, George A. *The Nature of Doctrine: Religion and Theology in a Postliberal Age.* Philadelphia: Westminster Press, 1984.

Locke, John. *The Reasonableness of Christianity with a Discourse of Miracles and Part of a Third Letter Concerning Toleration.* Ed. I.T. Ramsey. London: Adam and Charles Black, 1958.

Lohse, Bernhard. *A Short History of Christian Doctrine.* Trans. F. Ernest Stoeffler. Philadelphia: Fortress Press, 1966.

Lonergan, Bernard. *The Way to Nicea: The Dialectical Development of Trinitarian Theology.* Trans. Conn O'Donovan. Philadelphia: Westminster Press, 1967.

Long, A. A., and D. N. Sedley. *The Hellenistic Philosophers.* Vol. 1. New York: Cambridge University Press, 1987.

Luther, Martin. *D. Martin Luthers Werke. Kritische Gesamtausgabe.* 58 vols. Weimar: Bohlau, 1833-.

_____. *Lectures on Galatians.* Vol. 26 of *Luther's Works.* Ed. Jaroslav Pelikan. St. Louis: Concordia, 1963.

Macquarrie, John. *Principles of Christian Theology.* Rev. ed. London: SCM Press, 1977.

Maier, Gerhard. *The End of the Historical-Critical Method.* Trans. E. W. Leverenz and R. F. Norden. St. Louis: Concordia, 1977.

Marrou, H. I. *Time and Timeliness.* Trans. Violet Neville. New York: Sheed and Ward, 1969.

Mascall, E. L. *He Who Is: A Study in Traditonal Theism.* London: Longmans, Green and Company, 1945.

Maurice, Frederick Denison. *What is Revelation?* Cambridge: Macmillan, 1859.

Mays, James Luther. *Amos: A Commentary.* Old Testament Library Series. Philadelphia: Westminster Press, 1969.

McDonald, Lee Martin. *The Formation of the Christian Biblical Canon.* Nashville: Abingdon, 1988.

McDowell, Josh. *Evidence That Demands A Verdict.* San Bernardino CA: Campus Crusade for Christ (Here's Life Publishers), 1972.

_____. *More Evidence That Demands A Verdict.* San Bernardino CA: Campus Crusade for Christ (Here's Life Publishers), 1975.

McGill, Arthur. *Suffering: A Test of Theological Method*. Philadelphia: Westminster Press, 1968.

Metz, Johann Baptist. *Faith in History and Society: Toward A Practical Fundamental Theology*. London: Burns and Oates, 1980.

Moltmann, Jurgen. *The Crucified God*. Trans. R. A. Wilson and John Bowden. New York: Harper and Row, 1974.

_____. *Theology of Hope: On the Ground and Implications of a Christian Eschatology*. Trans. James W. Leitch. New York: Harper and Row, 1967.

_____. *The Trinity and the Kingdom: The Doctrine of God*. Trans. Margaret Kohl. San Francisco: Harper and Row, 1981.

Moran, Gabriel. "What Is Revelation?" *Theological Studies* 25 (1964): 217-31.

O'Connell, Kevin G. Review of *Introduction to the Old Testament as Scripture*, by B. S. Childs. *Biblical Archaeologist* 44 (1981): 187-88.

O'Donnell, John J. *Trinity and Temporality: The Christian Doctrine of God in the Light of Process Theology and the Theology of Hope*. Oxford: Oxford University Press, 1983.

Origen. *Die Grieschen Christlichen Schriftsteller der Ersten Drei Jahrhunderte: Origenes Werke*. Leipzig: J. C. Hinrichs, 1899–1976.

Osborne, Grant. *The Hermeneutical Spiral: A Comprehensive Introduction to Biblical Interpretation*. Downers Grove IL: InterVarsity Press, 1991.

Pelikan, Jaroslav. *The Christian Tradition*. 5 vols. Chicago: University of Chicago Press, 1971, 1974, 1978, 1984, and 1989.

_____. *Development of Christian Doctrine, Some Historical Prolegomena*. New Haven CT: Yale University Press, 1969.

Placher, William C. *Unapologetic Theology: A Christian Voice in a Pluralistic Conversation*. Louisville: Westminster/John Knox Press, 1989.

Pole, David. *The Later Philosophy of Wittgenstein*. London: Athlone Press, 1958.

Poling, James Newton. *The Abuse of Power: A Theological Problem*. Nashville TN: Abingdon, 1991.

Preller, Victor. *Divine Science and the Science of God: A Reformulation of Thomas Aquinas*. Princeton: Princeton University Press, 1967.

Quinn, Edward. "Revelation: Propositions or Encounter." *The Downside Review* 70 (1960-1961): 10-21.

Rahner, Karl. *Geist in Welt*. 2d ed. Munich: Kosel-Verlag, 1957.

_____. *The Trinity*. Trans. Joseph Donceel. New York: Herder and Herder, 1970.

Ramsey, Ian T. *Religious Language*. London: SCM Press, 1957.

Ricoeur, Paul. *The Conflict of Interpretations: Essays in Hermeneutics.* Ed. Don Ihde. Evanston IL: Northwestern University Press, 1974.

_____. *Essays on Biblical Interpretation.* Ed. Lewis S. Mudge. Philadelphia: Fortress Press, 1980.

_____. *Freud and Philosophy: An Essay on Interpretation.* Trans. Denis Savage. New Haven: Yale University Press, 1970.

_____. *Hermeneutics and the Human Sciences.* Trans. John B. Thompson. Cambridge: Cambridge University Press, 1981.

_____. *Interpretation Theory: Discourse and the Surplus of Meaning.* Fort Worth TX: Texas Christian University Press, 1976.

_____. *Time and Narrative.* 3 vols. Trans. Kathleen McLaughlin/ Blamey and David Pellauer. Chicago: University of Chicago Press, 1984, 1985, 1988.

Riekert, S. J. P. K. "Critical Research and the One Christian Canon Comprising Two Testaments." *The Relationship Between the Old and New Testament. Neotestamentica* 14. Proceedings of the Sixteenth Meeting of the New Testament Society of South Africa. N.p., 1980.

Robinson, John Mansley. *An Introduction to Early Greek Philosophy: The Chief Fragments and Ancient Testimony, with Connecting Commentary.* Boston: Houghton Mifflin, 1968.

Sanders, E. P. "Taking It All for Gospel." Review of *The New Testament as Canon: An Introduction,* by B. S. Childs. *Times Literary Supplement,* December 13, 1985, 1431.

Sanders, James A. *Canon and Community: A Guide to Canonical Criticism.* Philadelphia: Fortress Press, 1984.

_____. *From Sacred Story to Sacred Text.* Philadelphia: Fortress Press, 1987.

Scalise, Charles J. "Allegorical Flights of Fancy: The Problem of Origen's Exegesis." *Greek Orthodox Theological Review* 32 (1987): 69-87.

_____. "Canonical Hermeneutics: Childs and Barth." *Scottish Journal of Theology* (forthcoming).

_____. "Canonical Hermeneutics: The Theological Basis and Implications of the Thought of Brevard S. Childs." Ph.D. dissertation, The Southern Baptist Theological Seminary, 1987.

_____. "Origen and the *Sensus Literalis*". *Origen of Alexandria: His World and His Legacy.* Ed. Charles Kannengiesser and William L. Petersen. Notre Dame IN: University of Notre Dame Press, 1988, 117-29.

_____. "The Sensus Literalis' A Hermeneutical Key to Biblical Exegesis." *Scottish Journal of Theology* 42 (1989): 45-65.

Schaberg, Jane. *The Father, the Son, and the Holy Spirit: The Triadic Phrase in Matthew 28:19b.* Chico CA: Scholars Press, 1982.

Schilling, S. Paul. *God and Human Anguish*. Nashville TN: Abingdon, 1977.

Schillebeeckx, Edward. *Revelation and Theology*. Trans. N. D. Smith. London: Sheed and Ward, 1967.

Schleiermacher, Friedrich. *The Christian Faith*. 2 vols. Ed. H. R. Mackintosh and J. S. Stewart. New York: Harper and Row, 1963.

_____. *Hermeneutics: The Handwritten Manuscripts*. Trans. James Duke and Jack Forstman. Missoula MT: Scholars Press, 1977.

_____. *Speeches on Religion to Its Cultured Despisers*. Trans. John Oman. New York: Harper and Row, 1958.

Schrey, Heinz-Horst. *Existenz und Offenbarung*. Tubingen: J. C. B. Mohr, 1947.

Schweitzer, Albert. *The Quest of the Historical Jesus: A Critical Study of Its Progress from Reimarus to Wrede*. 3rd ed. Trans. W. Montgomery. London: Adam and Charles Black, 1954.

Sherry, Patrick. "Is Religion A 'Form of Life'?" *American Philosophical Quarterly*, 9 (1972): 159-167.

Stagg, Frank. *New Testament Theology*. Nashville TN: Broadman Press, 1962.

Steinmetz, David. "The Superiority of Precritical Exegesis." *Theology Today* 37 (1980): 27-38.

Sundberg, Albert C., Jr. "The 'Old Testament': A Christian Canon." *Catholic Biblical Quarterly* 30 (1968): 143-55.

_____. "The Old Testament in the Early Church (A Study of Canon)." *Harvard Theological Review* 51 (1958): 205-226.

_____. *The Old Testament of the Early Church*. Harvard Theological Studies, 20. Cambridge MA: Harvard University Press, 1964.

Sykes, Stephen. *The Identity of Christianity: Theologians and the Essence of Christianity*. London: S.P.C.K., 1984.

Tate, Marvin E. "The Old Testament Apocrypha and the Old Testament Canon." *Review and Expositor* 65 (1968): 339-56.

Temple, William. *Nature, Man and God*. London: Macmillan and Company, 1935.

Theophan the Recluse. "What Is Prayer?" *The Art of Prayer*. Compiled by Igumen Chariton of Valamo. Trans. E. Kadloubovsky and F. M. Palmer. Ed. Timothy Ware. London: Faber and Faber, 1966.

Thiemann, Ronald F. *Revelation and Theology: The Gospel as Narrated Promise*. Notre Dame IN: University of Notre Dame Press, 1985.

Thiselton, Anthony C. *The Two Horizons: New Testament Hermeneutics and Philosophical Description with Special Reference to Heidegger, Bultmann, Gadamer and Wittgenstein*. Exeter: Paternoster Press, 1980.

Tilley, Terrence. *Talking of God: An Introduction to Philosophical Analysis of Religious Language.* New York: Paulist Press, 1978.

Tillich, Paul. *Systematic Theology.* 3 vols. in 1. Chicago: University of Chicago Press, 1968.

Torjesen, Karen Jo. *Hermeneutical Procedure and Theological Method in Origen's Exegesis.* Berlin: Walter de Gruyter, 1986.

Toulmin, Stephen. *The Uses of Argument.* Cambridge: Cambridge University Press, 1958.

Tracy, David. *The Analogical Imagination: Christian Theology and the Culture of Pluralism.* New York: Crossroad, 1981.

_____. *Plurality and Ambiguity.* San Francisco: Harper and Row, 1987.

Turner, Ralph H. "The Self-Concept in Social Interation." In *The Self in Social Interaction.* Vol. 1. Ed. Chad Gordon and Kenneth J. Gergen. New York: John Wiley and Sons, 1968, 93-106.

Ugolnik, Anton. "The Art of Belonging." *Religion and Intellectual Life* 1 (1984): 113-27.

von Rad, Gerhard. *Old Testament Theology.* 2 vols. Trans. D. M. G. Stalker. New York: Harper and Row, 1962 and 1965.

Wainwright, Geoffrey. *Doxology: The Praise of God in Worship, Doctrine, and Life: A Systematic Theology.* New York: Oxford University Press, 1980.

Wallace, Mark I. *The Second Naivete: Barth, Ricoeur, and the New Yale Theology.* Studies in American Biblical Hermeneutics 6. Macon GA: Mercer University Press, 1990.

Warfield, Benjamin Breckinridge. *Revelation and Inspiration.* New York: Oxford University Press, 1927.

_____. *The Right of Systematic Theology.* Edinburgh: T. and T. Clark, 1897.

Whitehead, Alfred North. *Process and Reality: An Essay in Cosmology.* New York: MacMillan, 1929.

Wiles, Maurice. "In Defense of Arius." *Journal of Theological Studies* 13 (1962): 339-47.

_____. *The Remaking of Christian Doctrine.* Philadelphia: Westminster Press, 1978.

_____. *Working Papers in Doctrine.* London: SCM Press, 1976.

Wittgenstein, Ludwig. *Lectures and Conversations on Aesthetics, Psychology and Religious Belief.* Ed. Cyril Barrett. Oxford: Basil Blackwell, 1966.

_____. *Philosophische Untersuchungen/Philosophical Investigations.* Trans. G. E. M. Anscombe. Oxford: Basil Blackwell, 1963.

_____. *On Certainty.* Oxford: Basil Blackwell, 1969.

INDEX